EXPERIENCE
SPAIN

Spain is Europe's most passionate country. It is also one of Europe's most beautiful.

This is a country full of soul-stirring landscapes – arresting mountain ranges that rise like the ramparts of natural fortresses across the country, a coastline of unrivalled variety, backed by charming seaside villages, vast horizons and glorious beaches. Spain's natural beauty is sweeping and exceptional but it's not just for looking at. The options for exploring the natural realm are endless, from hiking the high country to snorkelling the Med with so much more in between.

There's no finer introduction to the Spanish soul than through its food. Food and wine are national obsessions here with good reason. The touchstones of Spanish cooking are deceptively simple: incalculable variety, strong traditions of recipes handed down through the generations, and an innate willingness to experiment and see what comes out of the kitchen-laboratory. You may experience the best dining ever over tapas in an earthy bar where everyone's shouting, or over a meal prepared by a celebrity chef in the refined surrounds of a Michelin-starred restaurant. Either way, the breadth of gastronomic experience that awaits you is superb.

Poignantly windswept Roman ruins, castles and cathedrals of rare power, and incomparable jewels of Islamic architecture also speak of a country where the great civilisations of history have always risen, fallen and left behind their indelible mark. More recently, what other country could produce such rebellious and relentlessly creative spirits as Salvador Dalí, Pablo Picasso and Antoni Gaudí and place them front and centre in public life?

For all such talk, this is a country that lives very much in the present. This book is, therefore, not broken up into sights or hotels or restaurants, or primarily into regions, but into five chapters that take you to the very epicentre of Spanish life:

→ **Tradition & Passion:** Flamenco, Food & Family

→ **The Good Things in Life:** Living la Buena Vida

→ **Living History:** Monuments of Art & Architecture

→ **Modernity:** Design, Style & Innovation in Spanish Life

→ **Adventure:** Exploring Wild Spain

Spain rewards those who visit in the spirit of full immersion and this book takes you into the heart of the Spanish experience. Perhaps you'll sense it along a crowded post-midnight street when all the world has come out to play. Or maybe that moment will come when a flamenco performer touches something deep in your soul. Whenever it occurs, you'll find yourself nodding in recognition: this is a place where anything can happen.

...and with that,
welcome to **Spain**

Left **Plaça d'Espanya**, Barcelona

3

Contents

People & Culture

The Spanish way of life

Above **Festes de la Mercè**, Barcelona

Spain wouldn't be Europe's most passionate country without the Spaniards. Animating this most animated of countries, Spain's people are passionate about all the right things. What other country could produce the fiery, uplifting, soul-stirring melancholy of flamenco, yet come up with festivals that poke fun at life with such infectious, casual élan? Where else on the planet could you find such heartfelt commitment to ancient identities that each seems to pull in its own direction, whether Basque, Catalan or Castilian, yet find such unifying passions for foods, artistic pursuits and sport? And what other country has so much fun doing it all?

Festivals fill Spain's calendar. There are sober religious affairs, none more so than the haunting Semana Santa (Easter) processions of hooded penitents. At other times, villagers jump over newborn babies in Castilla y León, everyone lets out their inner rage by pelting everyone else with tomatoes at La Tomatina, and fire lights up the night during Las Fallas in Valencia and Festes de la Mercè in Barcelona.

But Spaniards don't need a festival to get excited about life and indulge in behaviour that has as its main goal nothing more noble than an enduring love of having fun. Madrid's nightlife took on

Above Flamenco items

the quality of a myth during the 1980s when anything went and the world came to party. To this day, Madrid nights remain the stuff of legend. Perhaps there's something in the Mediterranean air that prompts extravagantly gay Sitges to not give a damn what the rest of the world thinks, while Ibiza just loves to party. The country's spirit is captured in those words that everyone in the world knows but which Spain and its people very much invented: fiesta and siesta.

Arts, History & Design

Fascinating past & innovative art

Spain is one of Europe's cultural power-houses. Down through the centuries, artists and architects have been the nation's storytellers on the world stage. From the time when the first peoples of pre-medieval Spain left their mark upon remote cave walls such as Altamira, art has been front and centre in Spanish life. Whether on canvas or in stone, some of Spain's most enduring attractions arose from the artistic sensibility that so enriched every era of the nation's history, from Roman Spain to the intricate splendour of Moorish Al-Andalus. This is the land of Velázquez and Goya, of Picasso and Dalí, of Gaudí and Cervantes. Art galleries, grand castles and cathedrals, even entire Spanish cities have benefited from the artistic vision that has prevailed here through the years, from Barcelona to Bilbao, Madrid, Córdoba, Seville and Granada.

A turbulent history has played its part. In seeking the prize of Spain, some of the great civilisations in European and world history left a lasting aesthetic legacy here. Roman sophistication lingers in architectural signposts and traces that echo through language, cuisine and even town planning. Enlightened Muslim rulers brought glistening architectural treasures and religious coexistence to a continent that seemed intent on tearing itself

Above Casa Batlló, Barcelona

apart. The violent European struggles for empire and the ebbs and flows of royal power, too, played out upon Spanish soil, and each era brought riches of different artistic flavour.

In the Spanish capacity for reinvention, in the nation's endless inter-mingling of the old with the new, there remains an ongoing dynamism to Spain's art and design. Across the genres, creative types from fashion designers and movie directors to Spain's flamenco artists and architects are writing an exciting new chapter in the fascinating story that is Spain's artistic heritage.

Food & Drink

Europe's culinary powerhouse

Above **Seafood paella**

Spanish food is one of the culinary world's most exciting stories, not to mention one of the most enjoyable reasons to visit the country. Food stands at the centre of Spanish living, at once a grand national passion and a touchstone of daily life. Whether at work or at play, Spaniards come together over a meal and generally agree that food is one of few things that unites this notoriously argumentative country.

Whether it's in the genius of tapas – going out for tapas (called *pintxos* in the Basque Country) is a recurring ritual among Spaniards – the splendid subtlety of *jamón,* the refinement of olive oil, the wonderful world of Spanish wines, or in the sheer perfection of paella, Spanish food is built upon the subtle interplay between tradition and innovation, between complexity and simplicity. As a starting point, the laws of traditional Spanish cooking are deceptively simple: take the freshest ingredients and interfere with them as little as possible. From there, anything is possible, and the infinite variety of food, drink and gastronomic experiences here is reason alone to visit.

Spaniards love to travel in their own country. They especially love to do so in pursuit of the perfect meal. Tell a Spaniard that you're on your way to a particular place and they're sure to start salivating

Above Sangría

at the mere thought of the local speciality and a favourite restaurant at which to enjoy it. That's because eating is more than a functional pastime to be squeezed between other more important tasks; it's a social event to be enjoyed with friends and one always taken seriously enough to have adequate hours allocated for the purpose. Following in their footsteps is one of life's great pleasures.

Experiences

Landscapes & Journeys

Diverse scenery that stirs the soul

Above Lloret de Mar, Costa Brava

Put simply, Spain is a land of astonishing variety and beauty. It is a realm of jagged mountain ranges that cordon off the peninsula from the rest of the continent like a protective shield and that rise as snow-capped peaks from parched, desert-like plains. It is a terrain of endless horizons that stirred the soul of poets and painters. And it is defined by an epic coastline, a nation encircled by near-perfect beaches, intimate Mediterranean coves, and cliffs that plunge into the Atlantic across the country's northwestern reaches.

Landscape as a beguiling natural backdrop to so many memorable travel moments is, of course, an essential element in Spain's considerable appeal. But Spain's scenery is so much more than window dressing. This is a country where exploration of wild places stands at its heart, a place where pilgrimages such as the Camino de Santiago traverse the contours of these splendid landscapes as much as they do the soul of a nation. Whether hiking or horse riding, cycling or surfing, Spain's landscapes provide both view and inspiration for getting out to explore. And it's not just about expending energy – there are endless possibilities for road trips, life-changing train journeys, and everything from spotting wildlife to watching the world go by from a picturesque Spanish beach.

Above Camino de Santiago

Spain's human story, too, seems to very much spring from the land that Spaniards inhabit. White villages cluster in valleys and colonise hilltops across Andalucía, stone villages serve as gateways to the natural stone fortress of the Pyrenees in Aragón, and the glorious Roman ruins of Extremadura stand at the crossroads of civilisations and ancient byways that still guide many journeys through the country to this day.

Experiences

A Day in Spain

Spain operates very much to its own schedule, and the late nights and unusually late meal times can take some getting used to for visitors.

The Spanish working day begins at home with breakfast, which is traditionally sweet – a pastry or croissant with coffee is typical. Work (and school) usually begins at 9am, although many shops don't open until 10am. Many workers break for a coffee and perhaps a snack mid-morning, around 10.30am.

Lunch is the main meal of the day. Although restaurants might open as early as 1pm, the normal time for lunch is 2pm or 2.30pm, even later on weekends or holidays. Tapas bars usually open earlier and many Spaniards will drop by for an aperitif – a pre-lunch tapa or two, and a drink. This is particularly common on weekends or during holiday periods. Although times are changing, most smaller shops close at 2pm and often don't reopen until late afternoon, usually 5pm, but sometimes 4pm. Larger shops usually stay open all day.

Lunch is a sit-down affair, consisting of a starter, a main and a dessert. Until recently, many Spaniards went home for lunch, usually followed by a siesta before returning to work late afternoon. The demands of modern life – in Spanish cities, few workers now live close to where they work, and most lunch breaks last only an hour – mean that this is often not possible these days. In the absence of a home-cooked meal, workers commonly eat in *casas de comidas,* simple restaurants that offer cheap, home-cooked, three-course meals, known as the *menu del día.*

Modern Spanish workers finish work around 5pm or 6pm, later for those who work in smaller shops, which often don't close until 8pm. Families with small children or those who have school the next day might eat earlier, but otherwise dinner – which, like lunch, may be preceded by an aperitif in a bar – rarely begins before 9pm and is often as late as 10pm or even later, especially on weekends. In cities, nightclubs rarely open before midnight, bars rarely close before 1am (3am on weekends), and many nightclubs stay open until dawn.

Experiences by Region

Northeast Spain

Above Park Güell, Barcelona

Irresistible Mediterranean appeal

Above **Sant Joan de Boí church**, Catalonia

The economic engine of the country, northeastern Spain is something of a world apart. Catalonia has always sought to assert its own identity, at times within the Spanish union, at times not, especially in recent decades. And yet, from here, and from Valencia, the Balearic Islands and Aragón, come so many characteristics that the world has come to know as quintessentially Spanish.

Valencia is less the home of paella than its birthplace, and is also known for its iconic festivals. The story of Spain and its powerful historical kings could not have happened without Sos del Rey Católico, located in the rolling, pre-Pyrenean hill country of Aragón and the 15th-century birthplace of Fernando II. For better or worse, Fernando II would, with Isabel, unite Spain, end seven centuries of Muslim occupation and cement Spain's Christian identity in perpetuity. And the essence of Spain's Mediterranean appeal – its balmy climate, its postcard-pretty beaches, its feel-good summers – very much resides in the country's northeast.

The irresistible energy of Spain's cities finds a highpoint in Barcelona, where architecture serves as a signpost to Spain's free-wheeling creativity in the city-wide creations of Antoni Gaudí. Food, too, dominates life here to the point of obsession. Barcelona is one serious food city in its own right with celebrity chefs, gastronomic societies and astonishing variety, drawing as it does on an extraordinarily rich landscape of *mar y montaña* (sea and mountains), of centuries-old traditions and a love of everything new. And it is in the hinterland, from the Pyrenees with their beautiful mountains and Romanesque churches to Salvador Dalí's zany legacy in the Costa Brava, that many of Spain's original attractions reside.

Spanish is spoken and universally understood in these parts, but you'll also hear Catalan (which can sound like a mix of Spanish, French and Italian) and a host of dialects up and down the Mediterranean coast.

Central Spain

Above **Gran Vía**, Madrid

Window to the Spanish soul

Welcome to the Spanish heartland. It was here in the Spanish interior, high atop the *meseta* (plateau) in what we now know as Castilla y Leon, Castilla-La Mancha, Extremadura and Madrid, that the Spanish character was forged. So many essential elements of Spanish culture spring from here, from the Castilian language itself to culinary mainstays such as roasted meats and hearty soups and stews, not to mention *manchego* cheese and some of the country's best *jamón* varieties, air-dried by the sere winds of the Spanish high country. This climate – bitterly cold winters, searingly hot summers – is so powerful that it dictates everything from the rhythms and seasons of daily life in the region to the food and character of the people. In the depths of winter, central Spain's inhabitants hunker down, taking refuge in their cities and villages and in their cuisine. Come summer, they evacuate to the beach.

Down through history, the kings of Castilla have held the line here, building a wonderful world of castles atop seemingly every rocky crag and fortress-like cities such Segovia and Toledo. When it came time in 1561 for a capital to be chosen for all eternity, Felipe II chose Madrid because he wanted 'a city fulfilling the function of a heart located in the middle of the body'. Across the Spanish interior, ancient stone villages that time forgot keep alive the traditions of Old Spain as a necessary counterpoint to the energy and drive that so distinguish the cities of contemporary Spain. More than anything else, it is this sense of history that defines the region.

Yes, there are Roman ruins across the region, and the architecture is very often sublime. But central Spain is no hoary old museum piece. This is also the land of Don Quixote, Cervantes' quirky literary creation for the ages, and of Madrid, one of the most dynamic cities on the planet.

Northwest Spain

Dramatic coastlines and unique cultures

Above **Squid with caramelised onion**

One of Spain's least-known corners, northwestern Spain – Galicia, Asturias, Cantabria, La Rioja and the Basque Country – is the antithesis of Spain's reputation for 'sun, sand and sangría'. Buffeted for the most part by strong Atlantic winds, Galicia in particular has an unpredictable climate of cold winters and sometimes disappointing summers. But there is nothing disappointing about finding so many experiences that you just don't find elsewhere, including Celtic cultural roots, dramatic cliffs and stunning fishing villages along Spain's most dramatic coastline, and food and festivals about which everyone else in Spain is known to salivate.

Food is a recurring theme up here. San Sebastián could lay claim to being Europe's favourite culinary capital, with more Michelin stars per capita attached to its restaurants than any other city on earth, quite apart from being utterly gorgeous as a stately relic from Europe's belle époque. The Basque love of food – creative *pintxos* (Basque tapas), steaks and seafood – sees food elevated to an art form. And perhaps more than any other region up here, the Basques see themselves as different and one look at their language alone – Basque is an ancient language with no known links to any other modern tongue – will tell you why. For all their tradition, the Basques and their neighbours in La Rioja pride themselves on that tradition–innovation seesaw that is such a feature in modern Spain. This is Spain's most creative culinary laboratory and Bilbao's Guggenheim is the architectural poster child for the New Spain, but the Basques will most likely sip on a time honoured Rioja red while they enjoy them.

Just across the provincial border, in Asturias and Cantabria, it's a land of cider and strong cheeses and hearty winter stews. The coastal villages here are intimate and as beautiful as any in Spain, cities like Gijón and Oviedo are up-and-coming artistic hubs, and the Picos de Europa could just be Europe's most arresting vertical sight, with hiking possibilities at every turn.

South Spain

Above **Arcos de la Frontera**

The cradle of quintessential Spain

Above **Cádiz**

If there is a region that most conforms to the Spanish stereotype, it's the country's south. Andalucía in particular is a world of whitewashed villages clinging to mountain perches – Ronda, Arcos de la Frontera and the other-worldy Alpujarras, for example – and cities of exotic architectural magnificence, most notably in Granada, Seville and Córdoba. There is something about a cobblestone street fronted by perfect whitewash and bedecked by cascading bougainvillea that screams 'Spain!' like few other images. Except perhaps the delicate horseshoe arches of Córdoba's Mezquita. Or the exquisite grandeur of Granada's Alhambra against the snow-capped backdrop of the Sierra Nevada. Or the orange trees and horse-drawn carriages and hanging *jamóns* in every bar in Seville. Baked by fierce summers and grateful for mild winters, Andalucía is a caricature of the Spanish experience.

Andalucía and its oft-forgotten neighbour Murcia are also large enough to offer up surprises, adding depth and variety to a journey here. Málaga is a Mediterranean city par excellence, rich in art galleries and a love of life Spanish-style. Carefree Cádiz just happens to be one of the oldest cities in Europe. And the region's wild landscapes are much underrated – the Sierra Nevada is brilliant for summer hiking and winter skiing, a network of protected parks receive few visitors, and wildlife, including the world's most endangered cat species, the charismatic Iberian lynx, as well as flamingos, inhabit pretty valleys and the world-class Parque Nacional de Doñana. Not far away, the triangle of Jerez de la Frontera, El Puerto de Santa María and Sanlúcar de Barrameda could just be the sherry capital of the world, not to mention the wellspring of flamenco, that most Spanish of musical genres.

They speak Spanish down here and are very proud to do so, but the southern version of the language can take some getting used to. In keeping with their relaxed approach to life, locals speak a casual form that often truncates words in a way that can be difficult for first-timers to understand.

Tradition & Passion

Flamenco, Food & Family

Steeped in tradition, passionate to its core, Spain is a country that wears its heart on its sleeve. You can zero in on any aspect of this country's limitless cultural variety – the quintessentially Spanish passion of flamenco, tapas, *tortilla de patatas* (the Spanish potato omelette that takes every Spaniard back to their grandmother's table), the ruby-red wines of La Rioja, the Camino de Santiago – and it's easy to see why Spaniards just love being Spanish.

Regional identities are, of course, a hugely significant part of Spanish life. Many who hold a Spanish passport actually consider themselves to be first and foremost Basques, Catalans or Gallegos (from Galicia). And yet, while rumblings for independence have occurred throughout Spanish history, these regional differences serve more often as a source of pride and tradition that adds to the glorious diversity of Spanish life. Food is one area where these identities assert themselves – then again, foods like *jamón* are a source of unity and are universally loved – but language, history and even architecture add to the joyous celebration of difference that so enlivens Spanish life.

The passions of the nation run especially wild whenever a festival falls. La Tomatina, that great tomato free-for-all in Buñol, might get all the attention, but who hasn't longed to join in? The eerie Easter processions might look like something from another age, but you can't deny that prickle at the back of your neck when masked devotees march in silence and ordinary Spaniards weep, moved uncontrollably. In the arts, too, Spain lives and breathes its passion for flamenco, the musical drama writ large that seems to flow from the theatrical heart of a nation.

¡Olé! Fiery Flamenco

Flamenco's spirit is clear to anyone who has heard its melancholic strains in the background of a crowded Spanish bar or during an uplifting live performance. At times flamenco can seem like an impenetrable world, but if you're lucky, you'll experience that moment when its raw passion and rhythm suddenly transport you to the emotial plane known as duende, *where joy and sorrow threaten to overwhelm you. If you do, you'll quickly become one of flamenco's lifelong devotees.*

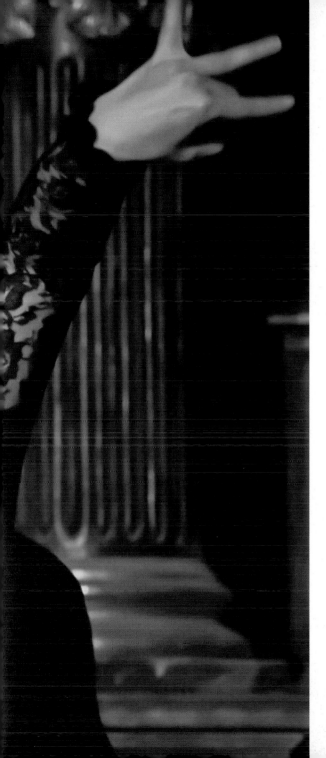

The Birth of Flamenco

The origins of flamenco are intriguingly vague. The long-time preserve of marginalised and culturally oppressed people (most of whom were illiterate), it was neither written about nor eulogised in its early days. Instead, the music was passed through bloodlines by word of mouth. No published testimonies exist before 1840.

The genesis of the art as we now know it took place in Andalucía sometime in the early 15th century, among disparate groups of Roma, Jews, Moors and perhaps other Spaniards. Anthropological evidence suggests that the Roma had begun a 400-year westward migration from the Indian subcontinent in the 11th century, settling all over Europe, with a southern contingent reaching Andalucía in the early 15th century. The Roma brought with them a dynamic form of musical expression – a way of performing that encouraged embellishment, virtuosity and improvisation – and they blended this rich musicality with the songs and melodies of the regions in which they settled. In Andalucía, they found natural allies among the Jews and Moors recently disenfranchised by the Reconquista (Christian reconquest). The collision of these three distinct cultures and the subsequent marinating of their music and culture over three or four centuries resulted in what we now know as *cante jondo* (pure flamenco).

The Essential Elements of Flamenco

One of the beauties of flamenco is its lack of straightforwardness. A handful of basic points offer some clarity. First, flamenco is an expressive art, incorporating more than just music. In the early days it was a realistic reflection of the lives of those who sang it – the oppressed – and they carried it with them everywhere: in the fields, at work, at home and in their famed *juergas* (Roma parties). Second, it is very much a 'live' spectacle and – for purists, at least – a necessarily spontaneous one. The preserve of the Roma until the 19th century, performances were never rehearsed or theatrical, and the best ones still aren't. Third, flamenco hinges on the interaction between its four basic elements: the *cante* (song), the *baile* (dance), the *toque* (guitar) and an oft-forgotten fourth element known as the *jaleo* (handclaps, shouts and audience participation/appreciation). The *cante* sits centre stage, as the guide. In its earliest incarnations, flamenco didn't have regular dancers, and guitars weren't added until the 19th century. In traditional flamenco performances, players warm up slowly, tuning their guitars and clearing their throats while the gathered people talk among themselves. It is up to the dancers and musicians to grab the audience's attention and gradually lure them in.

A flamenco singer is known as a *cantaor* (male) or *cantaora* (female); a dancer is a *bailaor* or *bailaora*. Most of the songs and dances are performed to a blood-rush of guitar from the *tocaor* or *tocaora* (male or female flamenco guitarist). Percussion is provided by tapping feet, clapping hands, the *cajón* (a box beaten with the hands) and sometimes castanets.

The traditional flamenco costumes – shawl, fan and long, frilly *bata de cola* (tail gown) for women, and flat Cordoban hats and tight black trousers for men – date from Andalucian fashions in the late 19th century.

Flamenco Through the Ages

Flamenco's 'golden age' began in the late 1840s and lasted until around 1915. In the space of 70 years, the music metamorphosed from an esoteric Roma art practised spontaneously at raucous *juergas* into a professional and increasingly popular form of public entertainment that merged *cante jondo* with other forms of Spanish folkloric music. It was during this fertile epoch that the modern musical forms took shape. Other innovations included the more complex choreography of flamenco dance and the emergence of the guitar as the de rigueur accompanying instrument.

The catalysts for change were the famous *cafés cantante* that took root in many Spanish cities, especially in Andalucía. The first cafe opened in Seville in 1842, and the establishments gradually spread, reaching their apex in the 1880s with prestigious venues such as the Café Silverio in Seville. Filled with mirrors, bullfighting posters, gilded stages and tables where patrons could enjoy alcoholic beverages, the cafes were the engine rooms of a dramatic musical cross-fertilisation not dissimilar to the blues-country fusion that later produced rock and roll.

Slide into Decadence

By 1920 pure flamenco, threatened by changing public tastes and impending political crises, was an endangered species. Fearing oblivion, Andalucian aesthetes Federico García Lorca and Manuel de Falla organised a competition in Granada in 1922 to try to save the art – the Concurso de Cante Jondo. But with the civil war approaching, the die was cast. The music entered an era known as

ópera flamenco, when *cante jondo* was diluted further by folk music, greater commercialisation and influences from Latin America. The controversial figure of the era was Pepe Marchena (1903–76), flamenco's first well-paid superstar, who broke with tradition by singing lighter *fandangos* and *cantes de ida y vuelta*, often backed by an orchestra. Purists were understandably leery, while others saw it as the natural evolution of a music that had leapt into the public domain. Just below the radar, *cante jondo* survived, in part because it was still performed by Roma singers such as Manuel Torre and La Niña de los Peines, the greatest male and female voices of their age.

Rebirth

The re-evaluation of *cante jondo* in the 1950s fell to Antonio Mairena (1909–83), an impassioned Roma *cantaor* from Seville province and the first real flamencologist to historically decipher the art. Mairena insisted on singing only old styles of *palos* (musical forms), many of which he rescued from almost certain extinction. Through his stubborn refusal to pander to commercial tastes, he provided a lifeline between the golden age and the revival that was to come.

By the 1960s, nascent *tablaos* – nightclubs staging professional flamenco shows – had filled the vacuum left by the closure of the *cafés cantante* in the 1920s. Some *tablaos,* particularly those in the new resort towns on the coast, were fake and insipid, while others played a role in re-establishing *cante jondo* alongside the newer *palos*. Flamenco's ultimate revival was spearheaded, however, not by venues but by the exciting performers who

frequented them. Two in particular stood out. Paco de Lucía from Algeciras was a guitarist so precocious that by age 14 he had absorbed everything any living musician could teach. His muse and foil was Camarón de la Isla, a Roma singer from the town of San Fernando (known as La Isla), who by the early 1970s had attained the kind of godlike status normally reserved for rock stars and bullfighters. Between them, Camarón and de Lucía took flamenco to a different level, injecting it with out-of-the-box innovations (such as electric guitars and keyboards) while, at the same time, carefully safeguarding its purity. Suddenly the rest of the world was sitting up and taking notice.

Flamenco Palos (Musical Forms)

The purist expression of flamenco, *cante jondo* (literally 'deep song') is a primitive collection of *palos* that includes *soleares* (a quintessential form with a strong, strict rhythm), the tragic and expressive *siguiriyas,* and *tientos, martineles* and *carceleras. Cante jondo* is considered to be the main building block of flamenco and good singers – whose gravelly, operatic voices can sound like a cross between Tom Waits and Pavarotti – are required to sing as if their lives depended upon it, and leave a piece of their soul in every stanza. The raw emotion and almost religious absorption of these powerful performers can be rather unnerving to the uninitiated. The ideal is to inspire *duende*. But *duende* can be elusive. Thus, it is up to the singer to summon it up, amalgamating yearning, superstition, anguish and fervour into a force that is both intimate and transcendental.

The other main grouping of flamenco songs is called *cantes chicos* (little songs),

palos that are more light-hearted and accessible derivatives of *cante jondo*. Popular *cantes chicos* are the upbeat *alegrías* from Cádiz, descended from sailor's jigs; the fast but tongue-in-cheek *bulerías* from Jerez; and the ubiquitous *tangos* made popular by the great Sevillan singer La Niña de los Peines.

A third, more nebulous, group of *palos* (sometimes called *cantes andaluces*) exists outside what most aficionados would call 'pure' flamenco. This consists mainly of *fandangos* that are descended from Spanish folk music, with each region broadcasting its own variation.

Seeing Flamenco

The intensity and spontaneity of flamenco have never translated well onto CDs or studio recordings. Instead, to raise the goosebumps and inspire the powerful emotional spirit of *duende,* you have to be there.

Seeing flamenco can be expensive. The admission price usually includes a drink, but you pay extra for further drinks or meals that aren't always worth the money. For that reason, it's recommended that you eat elsewhere and simply pay for the show (having bought tickets in advance). The other important thing to remember is that most of these shows are geared towards tourists. That's not to say that the quality isn't often top-notch – on the contrary, it's generally magnificent, spine-tingling stuff – it's just that the shows sometimes lack the genuine, raw emotion of real flamenco.

Local bars are your best bet to see flamenco on the cheap, although the music and dancing in these places is sometimes more akin to mad jamming sessions than

authentic *cante jondo*. Entry is usually free as long as you buy a drink. Well-known flamenco neighbourhoods such as Triana in Seville or Santiago in Jerez have a multitude of bars and are known as places where dancers and musicians come together to talk, drink and, if you're lucky, perform.

The best places for live performances are generally *peñas* (clubs where flamenco fans band together). The atmosphere in such places is authentic and at times very intimate, proof that flamenco feeds off an audience that knows its stuff.

To read about:
Horse Riding in Andalucía see page 148
Handmade in Madrid see page 270

Flamenco Festivals

Festivals are a great way to see fabulous live flamenco. Flamenco festivals attract the finest artists in the genre. The following are some of the best:

Festival de Jerez, Jerez de la Frontera (February–March)

Suma Flamenca, Madrid (June)

Noche Blanca del Flamenco, Córdoba (June)

Bienal de Flamenco, Seville (September)

Tapas:
The Flavours
of Spain

One of the world's most enjoyable ways to eat, tapas are as much a way of life as they are Spain's most accessible culinary superstar. These bite-sized bar snacks are the accompaniment to countless Spanish nights of revelry and come in seemingly endless variations.

Tapas fuse the ideas of a snack, a starter and the elements of a larger meal all in one – the secret to their success lies in this versatility. They can be the prelude to a more substantial meal, or the main event itself. They can be the tiny serving of food that miraculously appears whenever you order a drink, or they can be an entire menu given over to *raciones* – large plates of food to share.

In the Basque Country, tapas (or *pintxos* as they're known up north) consist of small slices of bread topped with all manner of niceties (anchovies, capsicum and croquettes are favourites) in various seductive combinations. In Barcelona, you're far more likely to be served high-quality seafood from a can. In Andalucía, expect the best *jamón* or fine Spanish olives. All of these – and all manner of variations in between – can be called tapas.

The History of Tapas

That an idea as simple as tapas could change gastronomic history is a mark of culinary genius. But where does the idea come from? One story – quoted most often in Andalucía, it must be said – asserts that the word *tapa* (which means 'lid' in Spanish) attained widespread usage in the early 20th century when King Alfonso XIII stopped at a beachside bar close to the southern city of Cádiz. When a strong gust of wind blew sand in the king's direction, so the story goes, a quick-witted waiter rushed to place a slice of *jamón* atop the king's glass of sherry. The king so much enjoyed the idea (and the *jamón*) that, wind or no wind, he ordered another 'lid' and the name stuck.

A different version goes back much further to another king named Alfonso

– Alfonso X in the 13th century – whose doctors advised him to accompany his wine-drinking between meals with small morsels of food. So enamoured was the monarch with the idea that he passed a law requiring all bars in Castilla to follow suit. Yet another legend attributes the birth of tapas to medieval Iberian inn-keepers who, concerned about drunken men on horseback setting out from their village, developed a tradition of putting a tapa of food atop each glass of wine or beer. The purpose was partly to keep the bugs out, but primarily to encourage people not to drink on an empty stomach.

Tapas serve a similar purpose today and may partly explain why the street-side bar and cafe culture of Spain is so civilised. And since Spaniards don't sit down to a main meal until late into the night, they need something to keep the conversation and wine flowing.

Types of Tapas

Tapas aren't so much the best represen-tatives of Spanish cuisine, but rather the most economically convenient export. The food in true tapas is humble, typically requiring minimal preparation (hence the abundance of cold meats, cheeses and pickles) – certainly not as fancy as some Spanish restaurants abroad will have you believe – yes, *pollo al ajillo* (garlic chicken) is a very typical Spanish dish, but you'll struggle to find a single bar that would offer it as a tapa anywhere in the Iberian Peninsula. Some bars will dish out small portions of *tortilla* (potato omelette), *magro con tomate* (pork with tomato) or *pipirrana* (tomato, pepper and onion sal-ad) as a tapa, but only because these can easily be produced en masse and stored in the fridge all day.

The variety of tapas is astonishing; the most common are basic Spanish cupboard-fillers such as olives (sometimes presented on skewers called *banderillas* alongside other pickles), nuts and crisps, followed closely by *tortilla de patatas* (hot or cold), sardines and other small fish, roast vegetables, *croquetas* and a long list of cold meats and cheeses served on top of slices of white bread.

Regional Variations

Inland Spain, with longer and colder winters, favours hot tapas such as *patatas bravas* (potatoes in spicy tomato sauce), *pimientos rellenos* (stuffed peppers), *calamares a la romana* (battered squid rings) or the aforementioned *croquetas*. The further south you go the more popular cold tapas such as *ensaladilla rusa* (Spanish potato salad) or *pipirrana* (tomato, pepper and onion salad) become. Likewise, the nearer you get to the coastline, the fishier your tapas will be, although *sardinillas en conserva* (pickled sardines) remain popular throughout Spain.

Gourmet Tapas

With the growth of mass tourism, the tapas tradition has evolved into an art of its own – but at a cost. These days, chefs like Ferran Adrià have elevated the concept into the upper echelons of Spanish gourmet food. Modern boutique restaurants push the envelope with more experimental tapas such as *pescadito frito con algas* (battered fish with seaweed) or *ensalada de naranja y zumo de oliva* (orange and olive juice salad). The price tag on these can easily match a standard main course in a Parisian bistro.

How to Order

Unless you speak Spanish, ordering tapas can seem like one of the dark arts of Spanish etiquette. Fear not – it's not as difficult as it first appears.

In the Basque Country, Zaragoza and many bars in Madrid, Barcelona and elsewhere, it couldn't be easier. With tapas varieties lined up along the bar, you either take a small plate and help yourself or point to the morsel you want. If you do this, it's customary to keep track of what you eat (by holding on to the toothpicks, for example) and then tell the bar staff how many you've had when it's time to pay. Otherwise, many places have a list of tapas, either on a menu or posted up behind the bar. If you can't choose, ask for '*la especialidad de la casa*' (the house speciality) and it's hard to go wrong.

In Andalucía, *tapeando* (going out for tapas) is a favourite pastime and, while it may serve as the prelude to lunch, it's often also the main event in the evening, when Andalucians drag out their evening meal with tapas and drinks. It's an ideal way to sample a range of tastes and specialities.

Etiquette

Tapas are generally volunteered but you will also find some Spanish customers, most likely regulars, who cheekily pose the question '*¿tienes alguna tapa?*' (have you got any tapas?), to try and wing a freebie. Pay attention to the answer: if the waiter nods and walks away, they will deliver the goodies. But if they start reciting the menu, it means they will charge you for whatever you choose. It's a subtle, but obvious, difference: you don't get to choose your free tapas, but if you pay you

are welcome to help yourself to the best of the menu. These paid portions are usually called *pinchos* (one to two portions) or *raciones* (a serving size for up to three people) to differentiate them from tapas.

To read about:
Jamón Jamón see page 48
Pintxos Route in the Basque Country see page 180

Bar de Tapas Tips

→ The best tapas times are from 1pm to 3pm and from 8pm onwards (9pm in summer).
→ Tapas bars are often clustered together, enabling bar-hopping between bites.
→ Ordering tapas is a physical contact sport; be prepared to elbow your way to the bar.
→ That massive crowd at the bar usually means something. Good tapas places aren't always fancy, but they're invariably crowded.
→ Don't worry about all those discarded serviettes on the floor – it's the Andalucian way to brush them off the table.
→ Granada, Almería and Jaén all offer a free tapa with every drink. Almería goes one better and allows you to choose which free tapa you would like.
→ You can also eat tapas as *medias raciones* (half-platters) or *raciones* (full platters).

Left *Calamares a la romana*

La Tomatina

Buñol's massive tomato-throwing festival, held in late August, must be one of the messiest get-togethers in the country. Thousands of people launch tonnes of tomatoes at one another in the space of an hour in an epic food battle.

Attracting more than 20,000 visitors to a town of just 9000 inhabitants, the mayhem of La Tomatina takes place on the town's main square and Calle del Cid. At around 9am a large greased pole with a ham attached to the end of it is hoisted into the air, and there's a mad scramble as people struggle against each other to pull it down. At precisely 11am, regardless of whether someone has successfully grabbed the ham (which is rare), a cannon is fired and more than 100 tonnes of ripe, squishy tomatoes are tipped from trucks to the waiting crowd. For the next hour, everyone joins in a frenzied, cheerful, anarchic tomato battle until a second cannon fire signals the end of play. Then it's a mad dash for the closest local wielding a garden hose.

The Backstory

The crazy food-fighting festival of La Tomatina began in 1945, but the reason has been lost to history. Locals have numerous theories, including the popular tale of disgruntled townsfolk attacking city councilmen during a town celebration. The true origin could be anything from an anti-Franco protest to simply a fun food fight between friends. Whichever way it started, the townsfolk of Buñol enjoyed the festival so much that it was repeated year after year. It was canned briefly during the 1950s for having no religious significance, but due to public pressure was approved in 1959 and has returned full-throttle every year since.

The festival is now held in honour of the town's patron saint, St Louis Bertrand, and the Mare de Déu dels Desemparats (Mother of God of the Defenceless).

Getting Involved

There are several ways to join the madness. Most people just come for the day, arriving on the morning train from Valencia and heading back in the afternoon. But if you want the full La Tomatina experience, stay in Buñol for the weeklong celebration, which involves music, dancing, parades and fireworks. The night before the fight, a paella-cooking competition is held, where women traditionally dress in white and men forego shirts altogether.

What to Bring

Plan your outfit: participants wear old clothes and shoes and might bring a pair of goggles to protect their eyes. A change of clothes is a good idea – most buses back to Valencia won't accept pulp-covered passengers.

What you don't bring to La Tomatina is also important. The crazed tomato-throwers take no prisoners; cameras are seen as positive invitations to pelt the owner.

Ensure tomatoes are squashed before you throw them to avoid injuring someone. But be warned that others won't always be so kind.

To read about:
Spain's Religious Festivals see page 60
Barcelona's Festes de la Mercè see page 256

Camino de Santiago Pilgrimage

'The door is open to all, to sick and healthy, not only to Catholics but also to pagans, Jews, heretics and vagabonds.' So goes the 13th-century poem describing the Camino de Santiago – the pilgrimage route that spans the Pyrenees, passes through forests, and traverses the wine and wheat fields of northern Spain, all the way to Santiago de Compostela.

The Camino de Santiago (Way of St James) originated as a medieval pilgrimage and, for more than 1000 years, people have taken up the Camino's age-old symbols – the scallop shell and staff – and set off on the adventure of a lifetime to the tomb of St James the Apostle, in Santiago de Compostela, in the Iberian Peninsula's far northwest. The Camino attracts pilgrims from every possible background, age and nationality: those religiously motivated, culture hounds, soul searchers, those longing for a great physical challenge, food and wine enthusiasts, and lovers of natural landscapes and the solitude of back roads.

Its allure dates back to the 9th century, when a religious hermit unearthed the tomb of James the Greater (the first apostle martyred – decapitated – by Herod Agrippa, in AD 44). The impact was instant and indelible: first a trickle, then a flood of Christian Europeans began to journey towards the setting sun in search of salvation. Santiago de Compostela became the most important destination for Christians, after Rome and Jerusalem. Its popularity increased with an 11th-century papal decree granting it Holy Year status: pilgrims could receive a plenary indulgence – a full remission of a lifetime's sins – during a Holy Year. These occur when Santiago's feast day (25 July) falls on a Sunday: the next one is in 2021. While the 11th and 12th centuries marked the heyday of the pilgrimage, the Reformation was devastating for Catholic pilgrimages, and by the 19th century, the Camino had nearly died out. But in the latter quarter of the 20th century the Camino experienced a remarkable renaissance. It was named as Europe's first 'premier cultural itinerary' in 1987 as people took to re-creating the medieval journey on foot and by bicycle (and, more rarely, on horseback).

The Ways of the Camino

There is no official starting point to the Camino, as over the centuries a web of routes arose across Europe, with pilgrims traipsing from various lands towards the reputed remains of St James.

The 'trail' is a mishmash of rural lanes, paved secondary roads and footpaths all strung together. Navigation is made easy, with yellow arrows on everything from telephone poles to rocks and trees. Scallop shells, stuck in cement markers or stylised on blue-and-yellow metal signs, also show the way. Along the path, twice a day, walkers have their Credencial del Peregrino (Pilgrim's Passport) stamped at churches, *refugios* (simple hostels), and even bars.

By far the most popular *camino* (path) is the Camino Francés, which originates in France, crosses the Pyrenees at Ronces-valles and then heads west for 775km across the regions of Navarra, La Rioja, Castilla y León and Galicia. From Ronces-valles the route takes roughly five weeks to walk or two weeks to cycle.

But this is by no means the only route, and the summer crowds along the Camino Francés have prompted some to look at alternative paths. In 2005, nearly 85% of walkers took the Camino Francés; by 2016 this had fallen to 63%. Four alterna-tive routes were added to the Camino de Santiago's Unesco World Heritage listing in 2015.

¡Buen Camino!

To the east of the final destination is the hilltop town of Sarria. Its cluster of medieval churches and convents signifies its historic role as an important stop on the Camino. It remains so today, a popular starting point for those wishing to cover the 100km minimum for a 'Compostela' certification. The steep street up to the Church of Salvador de Sarria is lined with restaurants offering 'Pilgrim menus' and shops selling hiking boots and walking poles worthy of a storybook wizard. They cater to a constant trickle of pilgrims: young people with esoteric tattoos and woven bandanas, and lone walkers of all ages with contemplative expressions. A few carry crosses, but most seem to be on a secular journey – a more common token, dangling by crimson thread from backpacks and wrists, are white scallop shells, the enduring symbol of St James, clapping like accidental castanets as they walk. Above the drone of bees can be

heard the greeting *'¡Buen Camino!'* (Have a good Camino!) as one walker passes another. The path continues mile after mile, through peaceful fields of wheat and corn, across busy streets and into warrens of medieval alleyways. From Monte do Gozo (Hill of Joy) the city of Santiago de Compostela is laid out in the distance, and there, jutting up above the skyline in elegant peaks, are the bell towers of the mighty cathedral.

Through the Porta do Camiño gateway, pilgrims step into the city's historical quarter. Millions of people have trodden the enormous granite slabs of this street, hemmed in by impressive stone houses and churches. In the tunnel staircase under the Archbishop's Palace, street musicians play a soundtrack to accompany the final steps into the magnificent cathedral square, the Praza do Obradoiro. Inside the cathedral, behind the main altar, is the Romanesque statue of St James. From here, pilgrims descend into the crypt and pay their respects to the apostle's relics. At the Oficina de Acogida de Peregrinos, one final stamp of ink in the Pilgrim's Passport confirms the journey's end.

To feel, absorb, smell and taste northern Spain's diversity, for a great physical challenge, for a unique perspective on rural and urban communities, and to meet intriguing travel companions, this is an incomparable walk. *'The door is open to all'*...so step on in.

Pilgrim Hostels

There are more than 300 *refugios* along the Camino Francés, and numerous *refugios* on the other *caminos*. These are owned by parishes, 'friends of the Camino' associations, private individuals, town

Left El Capricho de Gaudí, Comillas

halls and regional governments. While in the early days these places were run on donations and provided little more than hot water and a bed, today's pilgrims are charged €5 to €10 and expect showers, kitchens and washing machines. Some things haven't changed though – the *refugios* still operate on a first-come, first-served basis and are intended for those doing the Camino solely under their own steam.

Alternative Routes

Camino de la Costa/Camino del Norte From Irún along the coasts of the Basque Country, Cantabria and Asturias, then across Galicia to Santiago.

Camino Vasco-Riojano An alternative start to the Camino Francés, beginning in Irún.

Camino Primitivo Links the Camino del Norte (from Oviedo) with Melide along the main Camino Francés.

Camino Lebaniego From either Santander or San Vicente de la Barquera to the important Monasterio de Santo Toribio de Liébana in Cantabria; not actually a Camino de Santiago but part of the Unesco listing nonetheless.

Camino Portugués North to Santiago through Portugal.

Vía de la Plata From Andalucía north through Extremadura, Castilla y León and on to Galicia.

Beyond Santiago Many pilgrims carry on to the dramatic 'Land's End' outpost of Fisterra (Finisterre), an extra 88km, or Muxía (a further 30km still), which is considered sacred by pilgrims as it was

Tradition & Passion / 47

Essential Experiences

→ Standing on the French border at Puerto de Ibañeta (Roncesvalles), the same Pyrenean pass that Napoleon used to launch his 1802 occupation of Spain, and thinking about the long road ahead.
→ Sleeping in the *refugios* and *albergues*, operated especially for pilgrims by parishes, local governments, Camino associations and private owners.
→ Getting your Credencial del Peregrino (Pilgrim's Passport) stamped each day as you progress west.
→ Wandering through rolling, expansive stretches of vineyards in La Rioja, Spain's best-known wine region.
→ Admiring the sun filtering through the 1800 sq metres of stained-glass windows in León's Gothic cathedral.
→ Giving thanks for a safe journey at the altar of Santiago's cathedral.

here that the Virgin appeared (in a stone boat) before Santiago. Off the end of Fisterra's lighthouse, pilgrims burn stinking bits of clothing while watching the sun set over the endless blue abyss – there's nothing between here and America except ocean.

To read about:
On the Grapevine: La Rioja see page 50
Hiking the Powerful Pyrenees see page 200

Jamón Jamón

There is an oft-heard Spanish saying that 'in this country, we eat every part of the pig, except the walk'. There's no more iconic presence on the Spanish table than cured ham from the high plateau and the sight of jamones *hanging from the ceiling is one of Spain's most enduring images.*

According to legend, the Spanish passion for ham began with a noble Roman, Cato the Elder, who introduced it to Iberia through his tome *De Re Rustica*. There are many offshoots of his fine idea, among them chorizo, *salchichón* and *lomo*. But none has the prestige or pedigree of *jamón*. Unlike Italian prosciutto, Spanish *jamón* is a bold, deep red, well marbled with buttery fat. At its best, it smells like meat, the forest and the field, and is usually served sliced paper thin as tapas.

Spanish *jamón* (like wines and olive oil) is subject to a strict series of classifications. *Jamón serrano* refers to *jamón* made from white-coated pigs introduced to Spain in the 1950s. It was once salted and semi-dried by the cold, dry winds of the Spanish sierra, but most *jamón serrano* now goes through a similar process of curing and drying in a climate-controlled shed for around a year. *Jamón serrano* accounts for approximately 90% of cured ham in Spain.

Jamón ibérico – more expensive and generally regarded as the elite of Spanish hams – comes from a black-coated pig indigenous to the Iberian Peninsula and a descendant of the wild boar. Gastronomically, its star appeal is its ability to infiltrate fat into the muscle tissue, thus producing an especially well-marbled meat. If the pig gains at least 50% of its body weight during the acorn-eating season, it can be classified as *jamón ibérico de bellota,* the most sought-after designation for *jamón*.

The *jamones* from Salamanca (particularly around Guijelo) and the Andalucian province of Huelva (around Jabugo) are considered among Spain's finest. *Jamones* from Extremadura and the Teruel region of Aragón are also highly regarded.

The best-quality *jamón* is most commonly eaten as a starter or a *ración* (large tapa); on menus it's usually called a *tabla de jamón ibérico* (or *ibérico de bellota*). Cutting it is an art form and it should be sliced so wafer-thin as to be almost transparent. Spaniards almost always eat it with bread.

Cheaper types of *jamón* appear in a *bocadillo de jamón* (roll filled with *jamón*) or in small pieces in everything from *salmorejo cordobés* (a cold tomato-based soup from Córdoba) to *huevos rotos* (eggs and potatoes).

Another local version in Aragón is *las delicias de Teruel* (*jamón* served with toasted bread and fresh tomato).

To read about:
Tortilla: Spanish Omelette see page 66
Olive Oil: A Taste of Jaén see page 116

On the Grapevine: La Rioja

NORTHERN SPAIN **FOOD & DRINK**

La Rioja is to wine what the Basque Country is to food. It's the sort of place where you could spend weeks meandering along quiet roads in search of the finest drop. Picturesque villages, excellent wine museums, wine-centric festivals, bodegas offering tastings and vineyards stretching to the horizon make this Spain's most accessible wine region.

Harvest Time

By the time the late Spanish summer fades into early autumn, this medieval landscape of mountain and vineyard is spring-loaded like a trap. Everyone living in the region's tiny towns, scattered across the hills like pieces on a board game, looks to the skies, to the earth, to the colours of the vine leaves. They watch, listen and wait for the moment when the time and the fruit is finally ripe – for the moment when the wine ritual around which life in this area has been shaped for generations can begin again.

And then the signal comes – a combination of the weather, the condition of the soil and the colour of the leaves that nobody can quite put their finger on but which everyone recognises nonetheless – and La Rioja bursts into life. For the next few weeks, there's just one concern: getting every last grape picked as quickly as possible during the fleetingly short window of harvest time.

Legions of grape pickers sweep through the rows of vines like invading armies, brandishing knives and empty buckets. The rural serenity is interrupted by the sound of chugging tractors, pulling trailers laden with purple grapes from the vineyard to winery. The bodegas thrum and throb with the growl of machines ready to begin the time-honoured transformation from grape to glass, sending the sweet, pungent scent of crushed fruit wafting through the village streets.

During the harvest, everywhere you look, the landscape moves. The rise and fall of backs bending to cut the grapes; the sway of the vines being stripped of fruit; a flash of blue tarpaulin as a tractor weaves its cargo along the earth tracks.

And then, in just a week or two, the harvest will be over, and the bucolic landscape will return to quietude once more.

Towns & Villages of La Rioja

La Rioja, together with the surrounding areas of Navarra and the Basque

province of Álava, is Spain's best-regarded wine-producing region. La Rioja itself is further divided into three separate wine-producing areas: Rioja Alta, Rioja Baja and Rioja Alavesa. The principal grape of Rioja is the tempranillo, widely believed to be a mutant form of the pinot noir. Its wine is smooth and fruity, with hints of leather and cherries, seldom as dry as its supposed French counterpart.

The Riojans have had a long love affair with wine. There's evidence that both the Phoenicians and the Celtiberians produced and drank wine here and the earliest written evidence of grape cultivation in La Rioja dates to 873. Today, some 250 million litres of wine bursts forth from the grapes of La Rioja annually. Almost all of this (around 85%) is red wine, though some quality whites and rosés are also produced.

The humble grape has created great wealth for some of the settlements around La Rioja. Proof of this can be found in some of the extravagant bodegas and hotels that have sprung up in recent years in what otherwise appear to be modest farming communities.

Before hitting the wine road, it's helpful to learn a few basics: wine categories in La Rioja are termed Young, Crianza, Reserva and Gran Reserva. Young wines are in their first or second year and are inevitably a touch 'fresh'. Crianzas must have matured into their third year and have spent at least one year in the cask, followed by a few months resting in the bottle. Reservas pay homage to the best vintages and must mature for at least three full years in cask and bottle, with at least one year in the cask. Gran Reservas depend on the very best vintages and

Above Bodegas Ysios, Laguardia
Below Dinastía Vivanco, Briones

are matured for at least two years in the cask followed by three years in the bottle. These are the 'velvet' wines.

Logroño

Capital of La Rioja and Spain's wine-growing region par excellence, Logroño doesn't feel the need to be loud and brash. Instead it's a stately town with a heart of tree-studded squares, narrow streets, hidden corners and a monumentally good selection of *pintxos* (Basque tapas) bars. All up, this is the sort of place that you cannot help but feel contented in.

The superb Museo de la Rioja in the centre of Logroño takes you on a wild romp through Riojan history and culture – from the days when dinner was killed with arrows to re-creations of the kitchens that many a Spanish granny grew up using. The other major attraction is the Catedral de Santa María de la Redonda, which started life as a Gothic church before maturing into a full-blown cathedral in the 16th century.

Elciego

When the owner of the Bodegas Marqués de Riscal, in the village of Elciego, decided he wanted to create something special, he didn't hold back. The result is the spectacular Frank Gehry–designed Hotel Marqués de Riscal. Likened to the Museo Guggenheim Bilbao in architectural scale and ambition, the building is a flamboyant wave of multicoloured titanium sheets that stands in utter contrast to the village behind. If you want a closer look, the easiest option is to join one of the bodega's wine tours. You won't get inside the building, but you will get to see its exterior from some distance. A much closer look

can be obtained by booking a table at one of the two superb in-house restaurants or, if you've saved your pennies, by reserving a room for the night.

Briones

One man's dream has put the small, obscenely quaint village of Briones firmly on the Spanish wine and tourism map. The sunset-gold village crawls gently up a hillside and offers commanding views over the surrounding vine-carpeted plains. It's on these plains where you will find the fantastic Dinastía Vivanco. Over several floors you will learn all about the history and culture of wine and the various processes that go into its production. The treasures on display in the museum include Picasso-designed wine jugs, Roman and Byzantine mosaics, gold-draped, wine-inspired religious artefacts, and the world's largest collection of corkscrews. At the end of the museum tour you can enjoy some wine tasting and, by booking in advance, join a tour of the winery.

Haro

Despite its fame in the wine world, there's not much of a heady bouquet to Haro, but the town has a cheerful pace, and the compact old quarter has some intriguing alleyways with bars and wine shops aplenty. There are numerous bodegas in the vicinity of the town, some of which are open to visitors (almost always with advance reservation), including the welcoming Bodegas Muga, located just after the railway bridge on the way out of town.

Wine is more than on everyone's lips in Haro on 29 June each year when the otherwise mild-mannered citizens go temporarily berserk during the Batalla del Vino. In the names of San Juan, San Felices and San Pedro locals take to the streets with vino-loaded water pistols, buckets, bottles and even old boots to wage a 'wine war' in one of Spain's messiest play fights. To take part, you must wear a white shirt (it's compulsory) and expect to get completely and utterly drenched.

Laguardia

Ringed by high sandstone walls and accessed via huge wooden doors set within carved gates, Laguardia was once the last line of defence for the 10th-century Navarra kingdom. This explains why every hole-in-the-wall bar and cafe here has a cellar beneath it. Formerly used as bunkers, their size and cool temperature make these stone caverns obvious underground wine bars, perfect for a couple of quick *pintxos* – *morcilla* (blood sausage) with pimiento peppers, perhaps, or a small slice of bread piled high with goat's cheese, blackberry compote and walnuts – not to mention a glass or two of the local drop.

Just a couple of kilometres to the north of Laguardia is the Bodegas Ysios. Designed by Santiago Calatrava as a 'temple dedicated to wine', its wave-like roof, made of aluminium and cedar, seems to perpetually undulate like the digital signals of a heart monitor. Daily tours of the bodega are an excellent introduction to wine production.

There are several other, somewhat less confronting, wine cellars around Laguardia that can be visited, often with advance notice only – contact the tourist office in Laguardia for details.

Denominación de Origen

Spanish wine is subject to a complicated system of classification, similar to the ones used in France and Italy. If an area meets certain strict standards for a given period, covering all aspects of planting, cultivating and ageing, it receives Denominación de Origen (DO; Denomination of Origin) status. There are currently more than 60 DO-recognised wine-producing areas in Spain.

La Rioja is one of only two wine regions in Spain classed as Denominación de Origen Calificada (DOC), the highest grade and a guarantee that any wine labelled as such was produced according to strict regional standards. The second region given the honour is the small Priorat wine area in Catalonia. In Catalan the classification is known as Denominació d'Origen Qualificada (DOQ).

To read about:

Sipping Sherry in Jerez see page 94
Hiking the Powerful Pyrenees see page 200

La Familia

SPAIN-WIDE **PEOPLE & CULTURE**

For centuries family and religion were the cornerstones of Spanish existence. Religion may be on the wane, but family remains the pillar of life in this most community-minded of countries. Everything revolves around the nuclear and extended family, from the major rites of passage to the daily routines of the country's inhabitants.

Traditional Family Life

Traditionally, so many of life's most important moments in Spain took place in the warm embrace of the family. In old Spain, people often lived close to extended family members and meal times were communal affairs. Even people's work days and the opening hours of shops and other businesses were built around time spent with family, with all work pausing for two or three hours in the middle of the day for a lingering lunch at home and a siesta.

Modern Family Life

Daily routines have changed over the years as the country's working hours move towards a more pan-European schedule, although many smaller shops still maintain the same traditional hours. And with the rise of cities, people often cross town, taking up to an hour to get to work and another hour to get back home, making it impossible for the old ways to continue.

But what they are unable to accomplish during the week, Spaniards make up for on weekends and holidays. This is when the old routines kick in, including the long lunches in the company of family and friends, and the post-lunch siesta. Many Spaniards also spend weekends visiting relatives back home in the towns and villages where they were born. And generations of Spaniards remember with great fondness their long summer school holidays, spent with cousins and grandparents in their hometown villages, with working parents visiting on weekends. In summer, holidays by the beach in July or August remain an essential part of family life. And when Spanish families get together, it's typically a noisy, joyful affair, with everyone talking simultaneously and grandparents admonishing them for not eating enough.

Celebrations

Celebrations mark the most important landmarks of a Spaniard's life. Weddings are festive family events, transcending generations and drawing in people from distant corners of the family network. Many Spaniards marry in civil ceremonies, although church weddings remain common, but the reception, often hours later, is considered one of the most significant family events in a person's life.

And while fewer Spaniards consider themselves to be practising Catholics with each passing year, a significant proportion, even many who never otherwise attend church, still mark the most important Catholic rites – especially a child's baptism and their first communion. These events are primarily family affairs, held in restaurants and banquet halls. May is a particularly popular month for first communions.

The Changing Family

Although a significant proportion of young Spaniards have always remained at home long after leaving school, in recent decades this phenomenon has grown considerably. At first this was due in large part to the growing number choosing to postpone getting married. Until as recently as the 1990s, the average age of marriage was mid-twenties. Most now get married in their early to mid-thirties.

While this may initially have been driven by an increased focus on university study, careers and travel, Spain's difficult economic circumstances since 2008 have meant that many young Spaniards simply can't afford to move out of home. At the height of the decade-long *la crisis*, youth unemployment stood at close to 60%. Those that did have jobs often occupied low-paying positions – *mileuristas* became the label for those earning around €1000 a month – as wages stagnated, inflation climbed (including for rental properties) and interest rates rose. As a result, even those with steady jobs found themselves unable to survive without family assistance, with many postponing the decision to move out in the hope of better economic conditions to come.

With jobs at a premium, even for university graduates, the entire generation that came of age during the days of the economic crisis came to be known as Spain's Lost Generation. In some cases, this deepened family ties, ensuring extended families stayed together longer, but the pressure that came from financial difficulties also placed considerable strain upon many, with divorce rates on the rise. Significant numbers of Spaniards, both young and old, also emigrated elsewhere in Europe and beyond in search of opportunity.

To read about:
The Catalan Identity see page 68
La Siesta: The Art of Napping see page 86

Spain's Religious Festivals

Spain's best celebrations tend to revolve around religious holidays. From Seville's legendary Semana Santa (Holy Week) display to the bizarre Los Empalaos ('the Impaled') in Valverde, Spain celebrates its religious festivals with zeal.

SPAIN-WIDE FESTIVALS

Semana Santa in Seville

Only the *sevillanos* (citizens of Seville) could take the themes of grief and death and transform them into a jaw-dropping spectacle. Many cities around the world mark the Catholic feast of Holy Week, but none approach it with the verve and outright passion of Seville. Watch nightly processions led by various *hermandades* (brotherhoods), including hooded *nazarenos* (penitents) who shoulder elaborately decorated floats through the city streets in an atmosphere doused in emotion and religious significance.

Adding to the sombre atmosphere are the white robes and sinister conical hats the penitents wear – a look that was incongruously copied by America's Ku Klux Klan.

Romería del Rocío

Every Pentecost (Whitsunday) weekend, seven weeks after Easter, El Rocío transforms from a quiet backwater into an explosive mess of noise, colour and passion. This is the culmination of Spain's biggest religious pilgrimage, the Romería del Rocío, which draws up to a million joyous pilgrims.

The focus of all this revelry is the tiny image of Nuestra Señora del Rocío (Our Lady of El Rocío), which was found in a marshland tree by a hunter from Almonte village back in the 13th century. He attempted to take the statue home, but when he stopped for a rest, the Virgin magically returned to the tree. Before long, a chapel was built on the site of the tree and pilgrims started arriving.

Solemn is the last word you'd apply to this quintessentially Andalucian event. Participants dress in their finest Andalucian costume and sing, drink, dance, laugh and romance their way to El Rocío. Most belong to the 115 *hermandades* who arrive from towns all across southern Spain on foot, on horseback and in colourfully decorated covered wagons.

The weekend reaches an ecstatic climax in the very early hours of Monday. Members of the Almonte *hermandad,* who claim the Virgin as their own, barge into the church and bear her out on a float. Violent struggles ensue as others battle for the honour of carrying La Paloma Blanca (the White Dove). The crush and chaos are immense, but somehow the Virgin is carried round to each of the *hermandad* buildings before finally being returned to the church in the afternoon.

In recent years, Spaniards' rising concern for animal rights, spearheaded by animal-welfare political party PACMA, has drawn attention to mistreatment and neglect of animals, particularly horses and mules, during the Romería del Rocío festivities.

Misteri d'Elx

Every August, Elche, a small town in the Valencia region, stages an annual Unesco World Heritage–recognised play. A lyric

drama dating from the Middle Ages, the Misteri d'Elx is performed in the Basílica de Santa María. The mystery's two acts, *La Vespra* (the eve of the Virgin Mary's death) and *La Festa* (the celebration of her Assumption), are performed in Valenciano on 14 and 15 August respectively (with public rehearsals on the three previous days).

In even-numbered years, there's a single-day performance on 1 November, with two rehearsals in the days before.

One distant day, according to legend, a casket was washed up on Elche's Mediterranean shore. Inside was a statue of the Virgin and the Consueta, and the music and libretto of a mystery play describing Our Lady's death, assumption into heaven and coronation.

The story tells how the Virgin, realising that death is near, asks God to allow her to see the Apostles one last time. They arrive one by one from distant lands and, in their company, she dies at peace. Once received into paradise, she is crowned Queen of Heaven and Earth to swelling music, the ringing of bells, cheers all round and spectacular fireworks.

Los Empalaos

At midnight on Good Friday eve, Valverde hosts one of Spain's most bizarre religious festivities, Los Empalaos ('the Impaled'). Penitent locals strap their arms to a beam, their near-naked bodies wrapped tight with 60m-long cords from waist to fingertips. Barefoot, veiled, with two swords strapped to their backs and wearing crowns of thorns, these 'walking crucifixes' follow a painful Way of the Cross.

Iron chains hanging from the timber clank sinisterly as the penitents, dressed in white petticoats from the waist down,

Above & right **Fiesta de Moros y Cristianos**

make painful, silent progress through the crowds. Guided by *cirineos* (who pick them up should they fall), the *empalaos* occasionally cross paths. When this happens, they kneel and rise again to continue their laborious journey. Doctors stay on hand, as being so tightly strapped does nothing for blood circulation.

Moros y Cristianos

More than 80 towns and villages in the south of the Valencia region hold their own Fiesta de Moros y Cristianos (Moors and Christians Festival) every year to celebrate the Reconquista, the region's liberation from Muslim rule.

The biggest and best known is in the town of Alcoy (22 to 24 April), when hundreds of locals dress up in elaborate traditional costumes representing different 'factions' – Muslim and Christian soldiers, slaves, guild groups, town criers, heralds, bands – and march through the streets in colourful processions with mock battles. Processions converge upon Alcoy's main square and its huge, temporary wooden fortress. It's an exhilarating spectacle of sights and sounds.

Each town has its own variation on the format, steeped in traditions that allude to the events of the Reconquista. So, for example, Villena's festival (5 to 9 September) features night-time parades, while La Vila Joiosa (24 to 31 July), near Benidorm, re-enacts the landing of Muslim ships on the beaches. Some are as early as February, so you've a good chance of finding one whenever it is that you visit the region.

To read about:
Baby-Jumping Festival see page 146
Egg-splosive Flour War see page 210

Basque Culture

The Basques are different. They have inhabited their corner of Spain and France seemingly forever. While many aspects of their unique culture are hidden from prying eyes, the language, dress, sports and symbols of this special region are visible to any visitor.

Lauburu: Symbol of a Culture

The most visible symbol of Basque culture is *lauburu*, the Basque cross. The meaning of this symbol is lost – some say it represents the four old regions of the Basque Country, others that it represents spirit, life, consciousness and form – but today many regard it as a symbol of prosperity, hence its appearance in modern jewellery and above house doors. It also signifies life and death, and is found on old headstones.

Basque Language

Victor Hugo described the Basque language as a 'country', and it would be a rare Basque who'd disagree with him. The language, known as Euskara, is the oldest in Europe and has no known connection to any Indo-European languages. Suppressed by military dictator Francisco Franco, it was subsequently recognised as one of Spain's official languages, and has increasingly become the language of choice among young Basques.

Traditional Basque Games

The national sport of the Basque Country is *pelota basque,* and every village in the region has its own court – normally backing up against the village church. Pelota can be played in several different ways: bare-handed, with small wooden rackets, or with a long hand-basket called a *chistera,* with which the player can throw the ball at speeds of up to 300km/h. It's possible to see pelota matches throughout the region during summer. Other competitive sports include log cutting, stone lifting, bale tossing and tug of war, most of which stem from the day-to-day activities of the local farmers and fishers. Although technology has replaced the need to use most of these skills on a daily basis, the sports are kept alive at numerous fiestas.

Fiestas

To see traditional Basque culture in the flesh, there's no better place than at festivals. The daylight hours of most festivals are a good time to see traditional Basque dances: there are said to be more than 400, many of which have their own special kind of dress.

The most famous of the Basque festival events is Sanfermines, with its controversial *encierro* (running of the bulls) in Pamplona. The original purpose of the *encierro* was to transfer bulls from the corrals, where they would have spent the night, to the bullring where they would fight. Sometime in the 14th century someone worked out that the quickest and 'easiest' way to do this was to chase the bulls out of the corrals and into the ring. It was only a small step from that to the bloody and chaotic event that is still held in Pamplona every year.

To read about:
Pintxos Route in the Basque Country see page 180
Kalimotxo: A Summer Cocktail see page 186

Clockwise from top left **Peña scarf**, Sanfermines; **Man playing *pelota basque***; **Sanfermines procession**, Pamplona; *Lauburu* **symbol**

Tortilla: Spanish Omelette

SPAIN-WIDE FOOD & DRINK

It's so simple, just eggs and potato, yet here is a dish that will transport you to tapas heaven, rekindling your love affair with Spain, or making one inevitable.

Also known as *tortilla espagnola,* this omelette is really a potato frittata or 'egg-cake'. So, to be clear: gently sautéed sliced potatoes are bound together in the pan with a pour of seasoned, beaten egg. Cooked until firm, flipped (gently!), then hey presto, your egg-cake is ready.

There might be a few ways to enjoy Spanish omelette (served warm from the pan, or stashed in the fridge overnight and packed up for a picnic), but there's one setting that you just know is the right one in which to experience it: a bar, somewhere in Spain. It's midnight and the party is just starting. A glass of Rioja, or a beer, maybe both. Music, laughter...and tapas. And the quintessential tapas dish, Spanish omelette, appears in front of you, small cubes pierced with toothpicks, ready to fortify your stomach for a night of revelry. It's such a satisfying bite, firm and hearty in texture, honest and familiar in flavour, with the almost spongy eggs being the perfect carrier for the tender potatoes. Your challenge for the evening will be resisting the temptation to gorge.

What would an origin story be without apocrypha? Is it the genius of a Basque general during the siege of Bilbao, hitting on a cheap, hearty meal for the troops? Is it instead the same general ending up in a peasant woman's house and being served the simple dish? Or is it just solid peasant fare hailing from Pamplona? You know what – it tastes so good, the true origins of the Spanish omelette don't actually matter. Indulge whenever, however you can.

To read about:
The Perfect Paella see page 84
Churros y Chocolate see page 90

Tortilla

Serves 3 as a main or 8 as a tapa

Ingredients
→ 3 potatoes, peeled
→ ¼ cup olive oil
→ 4 eggs
→ ¼ tsp salt

Method

1 Slice the peeled potatoes into 5mm (¼in) rounds. Pour the olive oil into a pre-heated heavy frying pan and add the potatoes to the hot oil. Sauté the potatoes for about 10 minutes, until soft, then remove them from the frying pan and set aside on paper towel.

2 Whisk the eggs and salt in a bowl until thoroughly combined.

3 Add the potatoes to the egg mixture in the bowl. Pour the mixture into the still-hot frying pan. Cover the frying pan with a lid or heatproof plate.

4 Cook the omelette over a medium heat until the top is dry to the touch and firm. Turn out the omelette on to a plate. Slide the omelette back into the frying pan, top side down. Cook the omelette for another 1–2 minutes.

5 Turn off the heat and leave the omelette to cool slightly in the pan. Slide the omelette on to a board and cut it into bite-sized cubes. Spear each cube with a toothpick. Serve the Spanish omelette warm or cold, with your favourite beverage on the side.

The Catalan Identity

Like many European nations, the kingdom of Spain was cobbled together, by a series of conquests and dynastic alliances, from what were once separate states. Though the last of these was over 500 years ago, people in the peninsula still tend to identify more strongly with their ancestral village or local region than with the nation as a whole. With its own language, flag and local customs, Catalonia is quite distinct from the rest of Spain.

The fortunes of Catalonia have risen and fallen over the years, as Barcelona went from wealthy mercantile capital to a city of repression under the Franco regime, followed by the boom and bust of more recent years. Despite today's economic challenges, recent decades have seen Catalan culture flourish, reflected in the re-emergence of traditional festivals and dances, the prevalence of Catalan flags on many facades and the near-universal use of the Catalan language in public.

Parles Català?

For Catalans, their language is the key to their identity. Escape Barcelona and the Costa Brava's beaches and you'll find that *català* (Catalan) is all around you: menus and street signs are in Catalan, and it's often the only language spoken in villages. Written Catalan resembles both Spanish (Castilian) and French; its roots are in Latin and it's an Occitano-Romance language, stemming from medieval Provençal. It's spoken by more than 10 million people in Catalonia (both Spanish and French), the Balearics, Valencia (where it's called *valenciano*), Andorra (it's the national language) and Alghero in Sardinia. Having flourished in the 19th century, Catalan was severely suppressed under Franco, with books destroyed and the language banned from schools and public spaces, but since his death it has made a strong comeback and become an important focus of regional identity.

Today Catalonia's state school system uses Catalan as the language of instruction, though most Catalan speakers end up bilingual, particularly in urban areas. Around town, Catalan is the lingua franca: advertising is in Catalan, while newspapers, magazines and other publications can be found in both languages (though you'll find about twice as many options in Catalan as in Spanish).

The Catalan Flag

In Catalan folklore, the idea for the Catalan flag – alternating red and yellow bars – was born when, during battle, King Louis the Pious dipped four fingers into the wound of a dying Wilfred the Hairy, and ran them across Wilfred's golden shield. Never mind that Louis died long before Wilfred was born!

Festivals

Festes dedicated to Nostra Senyora de la Mercè (Our Lady of Mercy) and Santa Eulàlia – Barcelona's two patron saints – are the city's biggest bashes. You'll see plenty of *sardana* (Catalonia's folk dance) and human 'castles' (*castells*) being built there.

Folk Dancing

On weekends year-round, devotees of *sardana* gather in front of La Catedral in Barcelona, while a 10-piece band puts everyone in motion. Catalans of all ages come out for the dance, which takes place in a circle with dancers holding hands. Together they move right, back and then left, hopping, raising their arms and generally building momentum as the tempo picks up. All are welcome to join in, though you'll have to watch a few rounds to get the hang of it.

To read about:
Catalonia's Human Castles see page 70
A Catalan Food Trail see page 230

Catalonia's Human Castles

Among Catalonia's strangest spectacles are castells, *or human 'castles'. This sport originated in the 18th century in Valls, 20km north of Tarragona, but has since spread to other parts of the region. Teams of* castellers *clamber onto each other's shoulders, and then a daredevil child scrambles up the side of this human tower to perch at the top. The spectacle is a dramatic celebration of Catalan culture.*

The structure of the *castells* varies depending on their complexity. The *castell* starts with a *pinya,* a firm base of many interlocking bodies – anyone's welcome to join in – on which the tower will rise. Subsequent human tiers are formed by *castellers* who climb up in a specific order to raise the structure higher, usually between six and 10 levels. The *enxaneta,* the tower's pinnacle, is always a lightweight (and brave) child who must reach the top and signal with his or her hand. A *castell* is considered completely successful when it is loaded and unloaded without falling apart. The aim of the competition is simply to build the strongest, tallest and most complex tower of people, with men, women and children all competing. The highest *castell* in history was a 10-storey structure with three people in each storey.

The *castell* tradition has spread to other parts of Catalonia, but Tarragona's Festival de Santa Tecla is renowned for having the most dazzling displays. This colourful 10-day festival brings *castells* to Tarragona's centre. Watch the spectacle along Rambla Nova or Plaça de la Font, and stick around for the fireworks. Alternatively, Barcelona's Festes de la Mercè and Festes de Santa Eulàlia feature *castells* among the concerts, dancing, fireworks and general festival merriment.

To read about:
Gloriously Gay Sitges see page 190
Barcelona's Festes de la Mercè see page 256

Galicia's Celtic Roots

Galicia isn't quite a different country, but this distinctive north-west corner of Spain, separated from the rest of the nation by both geography and culture, is a far cry from stereotypical Spanish images. Galicia is a fascinating secret waiting to be explored.

Galician People

Galicians think of themselves as Celts, distinct from other Spaniards, tracing their origins to a wave of migration from the east in the first millennium BC, and earthwork forts from that period, known as *castros*, dot the landscape. Scenic Monte de Santa Trega in Galicia's far southwest corner offers the most spectacular examples of these relics.

The Galician language, *galego,* is, like Portuguese and Castilian Spanish, a Romance tongue derived from the colloquial Latin spoken in Roman times – but it also includes many words of non-Romance, Celtic origin.

Folk Music

Galician folk music has much in common with Celtic traditions in Brittany, Ireland and Scotland, and the haunting sounds of the *gaita* (bagpipe), violin, *bombo* (a big drum), flutes and the extraordinary *zanfona* (a vaguely accordion-like combined wind and string instrument) provide the soundtrack to many moments here.

The most sure-fire spot for hearing a Galician piper is the passageway between Praza do Obradoiro and Praza da Inmaculada in Santiago de Compostela, a day-long haunt of local folk buskers. The best place to catch a live group on a regular basis is Santiago's Casa das Crechas. Several Celtic music festivals liven up the summer months. The biggest and best is the four-day Festival Ortigueira at Ortigueira in the Rías Altas in mid-July, which attracts bands and musicians from several countries and tens of thousands of music lovers. Other annual festivals well worth seeking out include the Festival Intercéltico do Morrazo in Moaña (Ría de Vigo) on a weekend in July or August, and the Festa da Carballeira, on the first Saturday of August at Zas (Costa da Morte).

Leading *gaiteros* (bagpipers) and other folkies are popular heroes in Galicia. If you fancy tuning into this soulful, quintessentially Galician cultural scene, look for gigs by piper and multi-instrumentalist Carlos Núñez, pipers Xosé Manuel Budiño or Susana Seivane, violinist Begoña Riobó, piper/singer Mercedes Peón, singer Uxía, harpist and *zanfona*- and bouzouki-player Roi Casal, or groups Luar Na Lubre or Milladoiro.

Art in Stone

No whitewashed villages here. In these damp northern climes it's pure natural stone that stands up best to the elements. (Yes, Galicia's rainy reputation is justified – but you could easily strike

Right Galicians in carnival costumes, Verín

a warm sunny spell, and if you don't, the rain showers will often be spaced between sunny intervals.)

Two millennia ago, Galicians fortified the Roman town of Lucus Augusti (present-day Lugo) with a 2km circuit of stone walls with 85 towers that still stands strong today. Some 800 years ago a stonemason, known simply as Maestro Mateo, carved the portico of Santiago de Compostela Cathedral with 200 biblical sculptures that add up to one of the greatest works of Romanesque art. There's barely a village anywhere that isn't adorned by a little old stone church. Centuries-old manor houses dot the countryside, and some of them are now among Galicia's most delightful places to stay.

The roadsides are liberally decorated with pretty, carved-stone wayside crosses known as *cruceiros* – a distinctive Galician art form that reaches its highest expression in the 19th-century Cruceiro de Hío, delicately sculpted with key Christian scenes from Adam and Eve to the crucifixion. Stone grain stores *(hórreos)* on stone stilts are another picturesque feature of the countryside – the biggest *hórreo*, at Carnota, is 34.5m long.

Galician Gastronomy

You could be forgiven for thinking that nothing is more important to Galicians than food and drink. There are few things they enjoy talking about more, and even the media covers the subject in great depth: the quality of this year's chestnut crop, the wine that won the prize at the festival, the price of *percebes* (goose barnacles)...

Galician cooks and chefs take pride in putting an appetising dish on the table.

And with the fantastic seafood from the rocky coasts, the first-class fish brought in by Galicia's fishing fleets, and the high-quality meat from the inland pastures, it's hard to go wrong. Galician food bursts with variety and freshness, and chefs today are putting these exceptional raw materials together in endlessly original combinations of flavour and texture.

Then there's the wine. Though still little known, Galicia has five DOs (Denominaciones de Origen) producing top-quality wines, from the white albariños of Rías Baixas to the full-bodied mencía reds of Ribeira Sacra. And when it comes to beer, few would dispute that Estrella de Galicia leads the way among Spain's large brewers. Don't miss out on its 1906 special brew (bottled) or its unpasteurised *cerveza de bodega* (draught).

To read about:

Salamanca: The Golden City see page 108
Epic Rail Journeys see page 220

The Good Things in Life

Living la Buena Vida

Spaniards really know how to live. So infectious is their approach to life that many visitors to the country leave longing to return. You may wonder if the people of Spain really do enjoy life as much as they seem to; the answer, for the most part, is yes.

The ingredients for a happy life are remarkably similar to those that make up a memorable Spanish meal. Food here is at once a destination in its own right – every meal is taken seriously, so important is it to just about every Spaniard's day – and the sensory soundtrack to everything that Spaniards do and love. Take paella, for example. Bursting with flavour, it's the centrepiece of so many family and other social gatherings, a shared dish that just doesn't work for one. There's churros and chocolate, the ultimate Spanish comfort food that works for breakfast or dessert. There's zesty gazpacho that evokes the essence of the Spanish summer. And olive oil from Jaén is such a fixture in Spanish life that no meal is complete without it.

To think of these as foods alone misses the point. Each is a signifier to life as it's supposed to be lived.

A commitment to the aesthetics of public life is also central to Spain's *joie de vivre*. Andalucian courtyards in riotous colour or the golden sandstone of Salamanca are merely the most magnificent of many such adornments. A colonising of the streets for the singular purpose of having a good time, too, is utterly Spanish, as is the siesta, and making the most of glorious beaches. These aren't things that Spaniards do on their holidays, although they certainly do pursue these things with vigour at such times. This is how they live whenever they can all through the year.

Spanish Sands

Spain's beaches are Europe's favourite summer playground, but they're also a Spanish obsession – in August, the whole country hits the coast. And there's much more to Spain's coastline than the over-crowded Costa del Sol: rugged Mediterranean coves on Catalonia's Costa Brava and Andalucía's Cabo de Gata; wild sweeps of the Atlantic Costa de la Luz; spectacular, all-natural strands in the northwest; and blonde beauties gracing the Balearics.

Right Cala Marçal, Mallorca

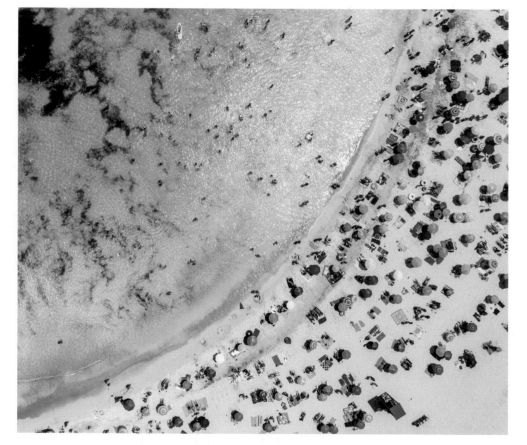

For Spaniards, a relaxing day at the beach (and it should typically last *all* day) is an excuse to gather the whole extended family together – complete with *tinto*-packed drinks coolers, jazzy deck chairs, home-cooked *tortilla de patatas* and, ideally, a carefully considered on-the-day booking for a leisurely lunch of deliciously fresh paella at a sand-side *chiringuito*. During summer months, especially August, it can feel like Spain's entire population has decamped to its many, multifaceted beaches – and that contagiously buzzy seaside vibe is half the fun for the throngs of foreign tourists who visit Spain each year (a cool 82 million in 2017, mostly British, German and French).

So it comes as something of a surprise that beach tourism in Spain has only been going strong for around half a century. Military dictator Francisco Franco began promoting tourism in the late 1950s, when Andalucía's original beach-holiday hotspot, the always-popular Costa del Sol, was born in Torremolinos (Málaga province), and tourism was developed along the striking Costa Brava in Catalonia. It wasn't until 1959, in Benidorm (Valencia), that bikinis were first legalised on Spanish beaches.

Today, despite Spain's unwavering summer popularity, its surfeit of coastal riches means that an unspoilt beach experience remains a real possibility – you just need to know where to look. The Mediterranean's gentle though touristed strands and pebbly coves contrast with the rougher beauty of the country's wind-lashed Atlantic beaches (whose snow-hued sands extend northwest from Tarifa to the Portuguese border, reeling in kitesurfers, windsurfers and sun-soakers); the dramatic,

Above Mallorca, Balearic Islands; **Right Platja de Blanes**, Costa Brava

Spain's Best Beaches

Trucador Peninsula With sugar-hued sands and perfect turquoise water, the beauty of this pencil-slim, natural-park-protected Formentera peninsula rivals that of the world's standout beaches.

Platja de Ses Salines A gorgeous strand of white Ibizan sand backed by glinting salt flats and sheltered by a natural park.

Punta Paloma A bleach-blonde Tarifa stretch bordered by dunes on Andalucía's undertouristed Costa de la Luz.

Platja de Migjorn Migjorn's snow-white sands sweep along southern Formentera, bathed by glittering-blue Balearic waters.

Fornells and Aiguablava These neighbouring Costa Brava coves near Begur are so divine it's difficult to choose between them.

Menorca Pick any golden-sand Balearic cove along Menorca's jagged coastline and you'll be blown away.

Illas Cíes Three spectacularly beautiful national-park islands wrapped by some of Galicia's most splendid sands.

Playa de Torimbia Clothing is optional at this shielded, honey-hued cove near Llanes (Asturias), accessed by foot.

Praia As Catedrais The other-worldly rock formations of this Galician strand near Ribadeo are such a drawcard that visitor numbers are limited.

Playa de la Concha A lovely scallop-shaped city beach at the heart of the Basque Country's San Sebastián.

cliff-strewn, less-visited northwest coasts of the Basque Country, Cantabria, Asturias and Galicia (home to a vibrant surf scene); and, far to the southwest, the sub-tropical beaches of the Canary Islands, loved for their year-round sun.

Costa de la Luz, Andalucía

Jazzed up by the colourful kites and sails of kitesurfers and windsurfers whizzing across aqua-tinted Atlantic waves, with Morocco looming just a few kilometres over the Strait of Gibraltar, the exquisite alabaster beaches that extend along the Costa de la Luz from laid-back Tarifa to cheerful, historical Cádiz are some of Andalucía's (and Spain's) most beautiful. Arriving on the Costa de la Luz from the Costa del Sol is like flinging open the window and breathing in glorious fresh air. Bereft of tacky resorts and unplanned development, this is a world of flat-capped farmers, grazing bulls, thrillingly located white villages, and glugs of dry sherry with lunchtime tapas.

It's by no means a secret these days, but Cádiz province's stunning Costa de la Luz remains the same old mellow beachy hang-out it's always been. Make like the Spaniards who, well aware of this, flock to places like Tarifa, Zahara de los Atunes, Los Caños de Meca and Vejer de la Frontera in July and August.

Ibiza & Formentera, Balearic Islands

These sister Mediterranean islands are blessed with a downright unfair number of fiercely beautiful sandy strands, many of which rival the world's finest beaches and are the key reason for the islands' astounding popularity. There are white-sand wonders where you can kick back in serious style and party until dawn at luxury beach clubs, as well as glorious un-developed stretches inside natural parks (head for Ses Salines and Es Cavallet in southern Ibiza, and the Trucador Penin-sula in northern Formentera).

Venture a little further and you'll find all kinds of impossibly pretty little coves dotted along the islands' coasts. Some of the most secluded and spectacular lie hidden away in northern Ibiza, where mellow Benirràs and cliff-flanked Aigües Blanques are famous for their bohemian crowd, and delightfully private wedges like Es Portitxol and Port de Ses Caletes will leave you wondering if party-hard Ibiza actually exists.

Costa Brava, Catalonia

Stretching north from Barcelona to the border with France, the Costa Brava ('rugged coast') is undoubtedly the most gorgeous of Spain's three main holiday coasts (the others being Andalucía's Cos-ta del Sol and Valencia's Costa Blanca). Though there's plenty of tourism devel-opment, this wonderfully scenic region also unveils pristine coves, unworldly seascapes, wind-battered headlands, coastal hiking paths, charming seaside towns with outstanding seafood restau-rants (seek out, especially, Cadaqués, Tamariu, Begur and Calella de Palafrugell) and some of Spain's best diving around the protected Illes Medes.

Cabo de Gata, Andalucía

Southeast from energetic Almería, the wildly beautiful Parque Natural de Cabo de Gata-Níjar protects some of Spain's most flawless and least-crowded beaches, encompassing 340 sq km of dramatic cliff-bound coastline and stark semi-desert terrain punctuated by remote white villages and isolated farmsteads. Besides beach-lazing, here you can go hiking, diving, snorkelling, kayaking, sailing, cycling, horse riding and 4WD or boat touring. The park, with its main hub in lively San José, stretches from Retamar in the west to Agua Amarga in the east.

To read about:
The Inland Beach: Playa de Gulpiyuri see page 218
Cabo de Gata see page 238

Clockwise from top left **Ibiza**; **Zahara de los Atunes**, Costa de la Luz; **Playa de Mónsul**, Cabo de Gata; **Playa de la Concha**, San Sebastián

The Perfect Paella

Paella was born in Valencia and it's in this sun-drenched city that the best, most authentic paellas are to be found. There's no meal better suited to an afternoon spent with friends overlooking the sea than this sumptuous rice dish, which somehow captures the essence of the Mediterranean table.

The problem with paella enjoying such fame, however, is that it can be extremely difficult to find a good one. Here are two tips for tracking down a paella as it should be cooked and served. First, stick your head in the door of a restaurant and listen – if Spanish or Catalan dominates the conversation, it might be worth sticking around. And at the first available opportunity, buy some saffron. Smell it. Its delicate yet pervasive aroma is unmistakeable and unforgettable. If that aroma isn't wafting up at you from the pan, you've been served a counterfeit. You'll find that in all but the better paella restaurants, saffron (which is extremely expensive) is often substituted with yellow dye number two.

The true *paella valenciana* is cooked with chicken, beans and sometimes rabbit, but more often you'll find the popular *paella de mariscos* (seafood paella) on menus. The base of a good paella always includes short-grain rice, garlic, parsley, olive oil and saffron. The best rice is the *bomba* variety, which expands in an accordion fashion when cooked, allowing for maximum absorption while remaining firm. Paella should be cooked in a large, shallow pan to enable maximum contact with the bottom of the pan, where most of the flavour resides. And for the final touch of authenticity, the grains on the bottom (and only on the bottom) of the paella should have a crunchy, savoury crust known as the *socarrat*.

For many of the Mediterranean seaboard's inhabitants, paella is just one rice dish among many. From Barcelona in the north to Murcia in the south and the Balearic Islands of Mallorca, Menorca and Ibiza out in the east, rice dishes (often served with lashings of aioli) are very often things of beauty and excellence. In the Balearics and Catalonia, they invariably arrive laden with seafood; a rice dish with lobster can be expensive but utterly magnificent, while *fideuà* (like paella but with noodles) is a Catalan variation on the theme. In Murcia, the rice is often served bathed in a rich stock with few other visible ingredients to distract you from the main event.

To read about:
Tapas: The Flavours of Spain see page 34
Gazpacho: Summertime Soup see page 96

La Siesta: The Art of Napping

Many societies enjoy a languid afternoon repose between lunch and early evening, but nowhere is the practice more culturally ingrained than Spain. The Spanish even have a word for their post-meridian slumber – la siesta – the two or three hours in the afternoon when the shops shut, the sun burns too hot for comfort and anyone with an ounce of Iberian spirit finds a place to lie down horizontally, close their eyes and benefit from a quick, rejuvenating nap.

The Rhythms of Spanish Life

Every country has its distinctive rhythms, a metaphoric clock that controls the ebb and flow of daily life. In Spain, the day revolves around the siesta. Traditionally, the Spanish tend to get up late, linger over lunch, slacken the pace in the afternoon and party boisterously in the small hours. A typical working day in Spain begins around 9am, stops for a two-hour lunc break and finishes around 8pm. Dinner is taken late. While restaurants in London and New York are packed to bursting at 6pm, the eating establishments of Madrid sit empty, or closed entirely, until 9pm.

Contrary to popular belief, the siesta tradition isn't just about napping; it incorporates a much wider middle-of-the-day slow-down that can be perplexing to unversed visitors. In most towns and cities, the bulk of small businesses pull down their shutters soon after the lunchtime rush and don't open them again until early evening (shops generally shut between 2pm and 5pm; restaurants between 4pm and 8pm). Stroll the streets of a small Andalucian settlement at 4pm and you'll likely find yourself in a veritable ghost town inhabited only by slinking cats and the odd tourist searching frantically for something to eat.

The Seeds of the Siesta Tradition

The Spanish didn't invent the siesta. Historical conjecture suggests that the Romans enthusiastically embraced afternoon naps. Indeed, the word siesta is said to derive from the Latin 'sextus' (sixth), alluding to the sixth hour of the day after dawn, supposedly the ideal time to retire for a bit of shut-eye, especially in Mediterranean countries where summer temperatures can be debilitatingly hot.

The anchor of the siesta is *la comida* (lunch). In Spain, the main meal of the day is traditionally taken late (2pm on average) and eaten slowly, accompanied by wine, conversation, family and a welcome spot of post-lunch lingering popularly known as *sobremesa*. To digest the large amounts of food, it makes perfect sense to grab a short snooze after your repast before heading back to work and slogging it out for a few more hours before a light, late *cena* (dinner).

Building on its Roman origins, the siesta was gradually adapted to accommodate the habits of pre-industrial agricultural workers determined to avoid grafting in the midday heat. But more modern influences have solidified the siesta as a central pillar in Spanish life. After the civil war in the 1930s, hard times forced many workers into having two jobs, one in the morning and another in the evening. An elongated siesta allowed them a brief respite between the two.

Equally influential was Spain's out-of-sync time zone. In 1942, the military dictator Francisco Franco bizarrely put the clocks forward one hour from GMT to CET (Central European Time) in solidarity with Nazi Germany. Instead of allying with Portugal and the UK, with whom it shares the same longitude, contemporary Spain sits in the same time zone as Germany and Italy much further to the east. During summer, it stays light until 11pm, encouraging the Spanish to stay up late, sleep less at night and thus be more in need of a mid-afternoon power-nap.

The Siesta & Modern Life

While ardent traditionalists argue the siesta is as Spanish as Don Quixote and shouldn't be tampered with, there are signs that the age-old custom is waning. By the early 21st century, over 60% of Spaniards stated that they rarely took an afternoon nap and numbers of non-siesta-ing workaholics are rising, particularly among young people in urban areas. Frenetic modern living and globalisation are both to blame. Long commutes, busy families juggling jobs with children, and standard nine-to-five business practices elsewhere in Europe simply don't gel with Spain's uniquely long and disjointed working day.

The topic has even entered the political fray. In 2016, then Spanish prime minister Mariano Rajoy announced plans to cut the Spanish working day to 6pm and switch the clocks back to GMT. The pledge was tinged with economic as well as political undertones. The Spanish don't just work longer hours than their European compatriots, they also sleep one hour less and, perhaps more alarmingly, are less productive. Although Rajoy's proposed laws are yet to be enacted, support for shrinking the siesta is growing, spearheaded primarily by business leaders.

Even if the stereotypical image of a straw-sucking farmer dozing under an olive tree is something of an anachronism these days, it's still difficult to see the siesta and all its knock-on traditions dying out any time soon. Napping aside, you can't change the whole rhythm of a country with one sweeping law. From Barcelona to Badajoz and from twenty-something millennials to greying baby-boomers, the Spanish are as attached to their

The Typical Spanish Day

8am Morning coffee on the run

9am Start work

10am *Almuerzo* (optional 'brunch', often just toast with crushed tomatoes)

2pm *La comida* (lunch) followed by *sobremesa* and a siesta

5pm *Merienda* (optional sweet afternoon snack)

8pm Finish work

9pm Tapas and/or light *cena* (dinner)

10pm *La movida* (late-night social scene)

12am and beyond Late-night churros (Spanish doughnuts)

post-meal *sobremesa* as the English are to their afternoon tea and the Italians to their evening *passeggiata* (stroll). Recent support for the siesta has come in the unlikely form of medical professionals, some of whom have suggested that a quick afternoon power-nap is not only inherently Spanish, but also good for your cardiovascular health. Long may it continue.

To read about:
Galicia's Celtic Roots see page 72
Barcelona Beyond the Crowds see page 250

Churros y Chocolate

Churros y chocolate *are a traditional Spanish breakfast treat: an irresistible dunking duo of mouth-watering dough-nuts, eaten piping hot and perfectly shaped to dip into the accompanying hot, thick chocolate. Not just for break-fast, churros are enjoyed during the early-evening* merienda *(snack) or while stumbling home from a night out at sunrise.*

Spanish churros are light, crispy dough-nuts made with a simple batter mix and quickly deep-fried before being immediately dipped either in sugar or dunked satisfyingly in a cup of thick hot chocolate. They are standard fare at every Spanish fiesta as well as being an essential component of a traditional Spanish breakfast.

Churros have humble nomadic origins. They were the traditional morning food of goat- and sheep-herders in Spain who, lacking any corner bakeries, whipped up a basic concoction of flour, water and oil to cook over an open fire. The churro is so-named after the horns of the churro breed of sheep reared in the grasslands of Castilla y León province. Chocolate (named after the Aztec word *xocolatl*) was brought from the New World back to Spain in the 16th century, where it was enjoyed as a drink long before it reached the rest of Europe.

Although a European-style doughnut may be the closest thing to a churro, the comparison really does this Spanish tastebud-treat no favours. One of the delights of the churro is that it is neither too sweet nor too doughy. Best enjoyed straight from the cauldron of bubbling oil, a reputable churro will strike you with just how crisp and light it is. Light, that is, until that fateful moment of dunking. Forget any preconceived notion of milky cocoa at bedtime, the hot chocolate here is so thick you can stand a churro up in it and so rich you will be spooning up the very last drop.

To read about:

Jamón Jamón see page 48
A Catalan Food Trail see page 230

Churros y Chocolate

Makes 20 churros

Ingredients

For the Churros
- → 2 cups plain flour
- → 1 tsp baking powder
- → 2 cups water
- → 1 tbs vegetable oil
- → ¼ tsp salt
- → olive or vegetable oil, for frying

For the Chocolate
- → 4 tsp cornflour
- → 4¼ cups milk
- → 2 cups grated dark chocolate

Method

1 To make the churros, sift the flour and baking powder together into a bowl.

2 Place the water, oil and salt in a large pan and bring to the boil.

3 Add the flour and baking powder gradually, stirring constantly with a wooden spoon, and reduce the heat. Continue stirring until a ball forms.

4 Remove the pan from the heat and leave the dough to cool.

5 Using a pastry bag or cake decorator with a 2cm (¾in) fluted nozzle, pipe the dough into strips around 10cm (4in) long onto a sheet of greaseproof paper.

6 Line a baking tray with sheets of paper towel.

7 Two-thirds fill a deep pan with oil and heat until a cube of bread browns in 45–60 seconds.

8 Fry a few churros at a time, turning once, until they are crisp and an even golden brown in colour.

9 Carefully lift out the churros with a slotted spoon and transfer to the paper towel to drain.

10 Repeat the process until all the churros are cooked.

11 Serve immediately or keep the churros warm by covering them with a clean dish towel while you make the chocolate.

12 To make the chocolate, combine the cornflour with a little of the milk in a small bowl.

13 Heat the remaining milk in a pan until it is hot but not boiling, then remove from the heat.

14 Whisk the cornflour paste and grated chocolate into the hot milk, until the chocolate is melted and the mixture is smooth.

15 Return the pan to the heat and gently heat the chocolate until the mixture has thickened slightly.

16 Pour into cups and serve immediately with the churros.

Legend & Luxury: Stay in a Parador

SPAIN-WIDE HISTORY

Sleeping like a king has never been easier than in Spain's state-run chain of paradores – often palatial, always supremely comfortable former castles, palaces, monasteries and convents. There are many dozens of them scattered across the country. Ranking among Europe's most atmospheric sleeping experiences, many are sited on prime real estate and prices are more reasonable than you might imagine. It's a wonderful way to experience the country's lavish past without the five-star price tag.

To read about:

Right **Parador de Santo Domingo de la Calzada**, La Rioja

Sipping Sherry in Jerez

In the sun-dappled vineyards of western Cádiz province, fortified white wine has been produced since Phoenician times, enjoyed by everyone from Christopher Columbus to Francis Drake. A distinctly Spanish product made for very British tastes, sherry is often considered a drink for English grannies. But now, sherry is making a comeback and wine lovers can dig deeper with tours, tastings, sherry-pairing menus and more.

Sherry, the unique wine of Andalucía, is Spain's national dram and is found in almost every bar, *tasca* (tapas bar) and restaurant in the land. Dry sherry, called *fino,* begins as a fairly ordinary white wine of the palomino grape, but it's 'fortified' with grape brandy. This stops fermentation and gives the wine taste and smell constituents that enable it to age into something sublime. It's taken as an *aperitivo* (aperitif) or as a table wine with seafood. *Amontillado* and *oloroso* are sweeter sherries, good for after dinner. *Manzanilla* is grown only in Sanlúcar de Barrameda near the coast in southwestern Andalucía and develops a slightly salty taste that's very appetising. It's possible to visit bodegas in Sanlúcar, as well as in Jerez de la Frontera and El Puerto de Santa María.

The Sherry Secret

Once sherry grapes have been harvested, they're pressed, and the resulting must is left to ferment in wooden barrels or, more commonly these days, in huge stainless-steel tanks. A frothy veil of *flor* (yeast) appears on the surface at the end of the fermentation, after which wines are fortified with a grape spirit, up to 15% for finer wines and 17% or 18% for coarser wines.

Next, wine enters the *solera* (from *suelo,* 'floor') ageing process. The most delicate palomino wines are biologically aged under *flor* (becoming *finos* and *manzanillas*), while coarser palomino wines are matured by oxidation (becoming *olorosos*); an *amontillado* or *palo cortado* is produced by a combination of biological and oxidative ageing. Wine from the sweeter grapes, Pedro Ximénez and moscatel, is matured through oxidation.

In the *solera* system, American-oak barrels, five-sixths full, are lined up in rows at least three barrels high. Those on the bottom contain the oldest wine. From these, about three times a year (more for *manzanilla)*, 10% to 15% of the wine is drawn out. This is replaced with the same amount from the barrels directly above, which is then replaced from the next layer – which means you'll never know quite how old your sherry is. The wines age for at least three years and may be refortified before bottling.

Jerez' Famous Old Tabancos

Sprinkled across the city centre, Jerez' famous old *tabancos* are, essentially, simple taverns serving sherry from the barrel. Most date from the early 20th century and, although the word *tabanco* comes from the fusion of *tabaco* (tobacco) and *estanco* (tobacco shop), the focus is indisputably the local plonk (ie sherry). In danger of dying out just a few years ago, Jerez' *tabancos* have sprung back to life as fashionable modern-day hang-outs, reinvigorated by keen new ownership and frequented by crowds of stylish young *jerezanos* as much as by old-timers. All are fantastic, cheap, down-to-earth places to get a real feel for Jerez – *fino* in hand.

To read about:

Gazpacho: Summertime Soup

ANDALUCÍA FOOD & DRINK

Like revenge, gazpacho is a dish best served cold; its icy medley of pounded vegetables, vinegar, olive oil and leftover bread is the perfect antidote to the Mediterranean heat.

In this country where seasons and climate play such a pivotal role in determining eating habits, Andalucía's climate looms larger than most. Summer arrives here with a ferocity unmatched elsewhere on the peninsula, especially in Seville, Córdoba and surrounding areas. While temperatures well above 40°C (100°F) may come as a shock to first-time visitors, locals learned long ago that there's no better way to keep cool than with a *gazpacho andaluz* (Andalucian gazpacho), a cold soup with many manifestations.

This is the sun-kissed taste of the Mediterranean countryside in a savoury smoothie. Its base is almost always a blended mix of tomatoes, capsicums, cucumber, garlic, breadcrumbs, oil and (sherry) vinegar. As well as climate, history played a significant role in its popularity here: it's a legacy of the New World, when Columbus brought back tomatoes and capsicums from his travels. It is sometimes served in a jug with ice cubes, with side dishes of chopped raw vegetables such as cucumber and onion.

Of course, you probably won't find gazpacho on offer in the cooler winter months, when warmth rather than a refreshing temperature is required.

Origins

Andalucians credit the invention of gazpacho to the Romans, though the Roman version came a few centuries too early to include tomatoes. This proto-gazpacho was most likely conceived as a way to use up stale bread in peasant kitchens, consisting of little more than old crusts, vinegar, water, olive oil and salt. In time,

the Romans left and Córdoba and Seville became the de facto home of gazpacho, spawning a host of vegetable variations.

The basis for modern gazpacho developed in Andalucía among the *jornaleros* (agricultural day labourers), who were given rations of oil and (often stale) bread, which they soaked in water to form the basis of a soup, adding the oil, garlic and whatever fresh vegetables were at hand. The ingredients were pounded together, and a refreshing and nourishing dish was made that would spread around the world.

Variations

Variations abound. A thicker version of gazpacho is *salmorejo cordobés*, a cold tomato-based soup from Córdoba where soaked bread is essential; it's served with bits of *jamón* and crumbled egg. *Ajo blanco* is a white gazpacho, a North African legacy, made with almonds, garlic and grapes instead of tomatoes. In Cádiz, sparse water supplies led to the creation of *arranque roteño*, so thick it could almost be a dip. In Extremadura, hunks of ham are added to the mix. To be truly authentic, any gazpacho should be pounded with a pestle and mortar to release the flavours.

To read about:
Tapas: The Flavours of Spain see page 34
Horse Riding in Andalucía see page 148

Gazpacho

Ingredients
→ 2 garlic cloves, peeled and diced
→ 1 red onion, peeled and diced
→ 1 red capsicum, deseeded and diced
→ ½ cucumber, diced
→ 500g ripe plum (roma) tomatoes, diced
→ 100g stale crusty white bread, broken into small chunks
→ salt and ground black pepper, to taste
→ 4 tbs olive oil
→ 1 cup passata
→ 4 tbs sherry vinegar
→ 1 tsp sugar

Method
1 Place diced garlic, onion, capsicum, cucumber and tomatoes together in a large bowl.

2 Add the bread and season with salt and pepper, to taste.

3 Add the olive oil, passata, sherry vinegar and sugar.

4 Squeeze the mixture together with your hands to blend the flavours.

5 Cover and place in the fridge overnight to chill.

6 Remove from the fridge and pound the mixture in a pestle and mortar, to make a smooth mix.

7 Return to the fridge until ready to serve.

8 Serve with toasted crusty white bread, brushed with olive oil and seasoned with salt and pepper.

The Mountains of Picos de Europa

NORTHERN SPAIN LANDSCAPES

The jagged, deeply fissured Picos de Europa straddle southeast Asturias, southwest Cantabria and northern Castilla y León, offering some of Spain's finest walking country – and some of Europe's most spectacular mountain scenery. Though the name (Peaks of Europe) might seem presumptuously grand, this northern Spanish national park lives up to its billing.

First sunlight begins its slow cascade down the mountains, spilling into a dusky lake below. As the sky brightens, white peaks and rocky foothills are doubled in the water's surface. A scattered herd of honey-haired Casín cows wanders up a grassy hill nearby, bells clanking heavily.

Lago de la Ercina is one of the Lagos de Covadonga, two beautiful glacial lakes set in the midst of the karst mountain range, which stretches out in three jagged massifs. It is said the name of the range originated with Spanish sailors returning from the Americas – the jagged peaks their first glimpse of land across the Atlantic.

This is the place where the Spanish Reconquista (Christian reconquest) started 1300 years ago, and just a few kilometres away a brown bear could be taking a nap. If that doesn't make you take note, then some of the mouth-numbingly strong Cabrales cheese and the local firewater, *orujo,* should do the trick. The Picos de Europa mountains pack history, activities, wildlife and culture into a small space.

In the early 8th century the area was the stronghold for Pelayo and his band of Visigoths who, against the odds, defeated the invading Moors and established a Christian kingdom here. Today, the park is a refuge of a different kind – endangered species like the Cantabrian brown bear and the Iberian wolf hide among the green folds between the peaks, as do Pyrenean chamois and an array of amphibians and birds, including the reintroduced lammergeier (bearded vulture). Easier to spot are the hikers, as they move around a criss-crossing network of 35 well-signposted hiking trails, ranging from easy ambles to demanding high-mountain routes. They tramp through forest glades where yellow and purple wildflowers grow between stands of chestnut and bushy holm oak, and up into narrow mountain pathways.

Sweeping past the hikers are cyclists, from lycra-clad enthusiasts to puffing day trippers, standing on their pedals and pumping their legs like pistons along stretches of road that trace the mountain curves, revealing views over distant peaks that seem to bob up from misty basins. The road up to the lakes is unforgiving, a climb to more than 1000m – the descent is more fun. Every few minutes a bike zips by, soon to arrive at the foot of the twin-spired basilica, Our Lady of Covadonga.

The Picos are run through by three rivers, creating valleys and ravines including the famous – and famously popular – Garganta del Cares, a steep gorge flanked by cliffs. Below, the Río Cares carves through the landscape, bringing with it

Right **Lago de la Ercina**, Asturias

small shoals of canoes and kayaks, their occupants barely paddling as they ride the current.

For locals, there's only one activity worth pursuing: climbing. It is considered to be in the blood – a shared genetic predisposition to be as sure-footed as a mountain goat. El Naranjo de Bulnes is the most challenging of the Picos and the region's best-known peak, with a distinctive shape and a name that translates to the Orange Tree of Bulnes village. For a lammergeier's view of the southern Picos without the climbing, the Fuente Dé cable car offers an easier way of getting up in the clouds, whisking passengers up an ear-popping 753m in just four minutes to soak up the spectacular views.

Whether you walk, cycle, kayak or climb your way through one of Europe's most striking landscapes, evenings are best spent enjoying dinner in one of the Picos' pretty villages. For a true Picos experience, wash down the local Cabrales cheese with some tangy Asturian cider while recounting tales of bear-paw prints and blisters.

To read about:
Hiking the Powerful Pyrenees see page 200
Call of the Wild see page 204

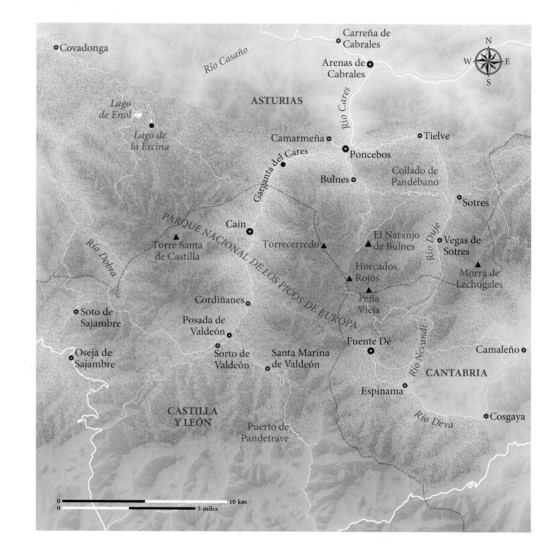

Walking the Garganta del Cares

Traversed by the Río Cares, the magnificent 1km-deep, 10km-long Garganta del Cares gorge separates the Picos' western massif from its central sibling. This dramatic limestone canyon extends between Poncebos, 6km south of Arenas de Cabrales in Asturias, and Caín in Castilla y León. People flock here year-round, but especially in summer, to walk the insanely popular Ruta del Cares, carved high into and through the rugged walls of the gorge between the two villages.

You can walk Spain's favourite trail in either direction, but head from north (Poncebos) to south (Caín) to save its finest stretches for last. If you're feeling fit, it's quite possible to walk the whole 10km and return in one (somewhat tiring) day's outing; it takes six to seven hours plus stops.

Left Garganta del Cares

Chasing Cheese & Cider in Asturias

ASTURIAS **FOOD & DRINK**

Done the tapas thing? Drunk the cerveza? How about trying a piece of Spain with unique flavours and intimate gastronomic experiences, right beside some of the country's most spectacular mountain scenery? Welcome to the Cabrales region of Asturias.

Asturian cider is served *escanciada*, poured like a waterfall from a bottle held high overhead into a glass held low, which gives it the required fizz. As the cider hits the glass it foams and bubbles like a sorcerer's potion, though the sound can only just be heard over the hubbub of a weekend evening on the cobblestones of Arenas de Cabrales' main square. Don't worry, you don't have to pour it yourself – bar staff will flaunt their skills by not even looking at the glass or bottle as they pour, probably chatting to somebody else over their shoulder at the same time. A shot of cider, about one-fifth of a glass, is known as a *culete* or *culín*; immediately knock it back in one go (leaving a tiny bit in the glass), before the fizz dissipates.

All around the square, similar apple waterfalls pour into glasses as the ritual of cider tasting continues. It's a time-honoured tradition in this region that produces around 80% of Spanish cider – anything up to 30 million litres a year, depending on the apple harvest. About 95% of this is consumed in Asturias itself. Apples are reaped in autumn and crushed to a pulp (about three-quarters of which winds up as apple juice). The cider is fermented in *pipes* (barrels) over winter. It takes about 800kg of apples to fill a 450L *pipa,* which makes 600 bottles. Traditionally, the *pipes* were transported to *chigres* (cider taverns) and drinkers would be served direct from the *pipa*. The *chigre* is dying out, though, and most cider now comes in bottles in *sidrerías* (cider bars).

Every Asturian town has plenty of *sidrerías* but the epicentre of the scene is Oviedo's *El bulevar de la sidra,* lined with a dozen jam-packed *sidrerías*.

Toasts – *salud!* – are cried, and then the cider is quickly poured long and strong down thirsty throats. On each table, plates are arrayed in a sea of tapas. There are black puddings, brochettes and, naturally, Cabrales' other star culinary attraction: its wonderful cheese, veined with natural blue-green moulds (similar in style to the famed Roquefort cheeses of France) from the caves that puncture the limestone Picos de Europa.

It's clear that time has moved on in Asturias and Cabrales. Once considered an epicurean black hole between the famed *pintxos* (Basque tapas) of San Sebastián and the *pulperias* (octopus restaurants) of Galicia, it was a place of peasantry, where the food – *fabada* (bean stew), sausage, chorizo – was typically as solid and unadulterated as its mountains. In the squares and *sidrerías* of Cabrales, however, you can

Right Cabrales cheese

see that this land of cheese and cider is as enticing as the metaphoric land of milk and honey. It's an experience to drink to.

In Cabrales it's said that the higher the village, the better the cheese. And there's no higher village than Sotres. At the edge of the village, with its steep, winding lanes and stone houses, you'll find Quesería Maín, a cheesemaking operation that produces some of the finest cheese around.

It's low-key and simple, but drop-in visitors are welcome; ask at the Hotel Sotres. Inside the *quesería,* the cheesemaker prepares the curds, drying them for two to three weeks in a refrigerated room before moving them into the Picos de Europa's caves – natural caves that are still used for maturing cheese. The highest cave sits at 1600m – requiring a two-hour walk – where the temperature lingers at around 6°C (43°F), and the air is thick with humidity and the pungency of cheese.

Across the valley, in hilltop Asiego, you'll find an equally personal gastronomic experience on the Ruta'l Quesu y la Sidra (Cheese and Cider Route). Here, a local cider maker leads guests on a two-hour walk into a cheese cave and through 20 hectares of apple orchards, from where 10 varieties of apple are blended to create ciders at the small Sidrería Niembro. It's at the sidrería, among Asiego's narrow medieval streets, that you'll finish your stroll. Depending on the season, there may be apples being pressed or bottled around you (the fruit is collected in October and November), while at any time of year there'll be a mouthwatering tapas meal over which to linger.

Above *Sidrería*, Santillana del Mar; **Right Pouring cider**, Gijón

To read about:
Tapas: The Flavours of Spain see page 34
The Hour of Vermouth see page 272

Essential Experiences

→ Being assaulted by the scent of maturing cheese as you step down into one of the Picos de Europa's cheese caves.

→ Saluting the good life as you enter into the *culín* spirit in one of Asturias' many bars or *sidrerías*.

→ Mingling with the cheese's source as you wander through the cows around the grassy Col Pandebano in the Picos de Europa.

→ Paying homage at the Museo de la Sidra (Cider Museum) in Nava, Asturias' biggest cider-production centre; come in July for the Festival de la Sidra Natural.

→ Finding the perfect blend of cheese and cider on the Ruta'l Quesu y la Sidra (Cheese and Cider Route).

Córdoba's Patios in Bloom

ANDALUCÍA ART & ARCHITECTURE

Paradise, according to Islamic tradition, is a garden. It's an idea that architects took to heart during Moorish times and later, surrounding some of Andalucía's loveliest buildings with abundant colour and fragrance. Studded with pots of geraniums, with bougainvillea cascading down the walls and a trickling fountain in the middle, the famed patios of Córdoba have provided shade during the searing heat of summer for centuries.

The origin of these much-loved courtyards probably lies in the Roman atrium (open spaces inside buildings). The tradition was continued by the Arabs, for whom the internal courtyard was an area where women went about their family life and household jobs. The addition of a central fountain and multitudes of plants heightened the sensation of coolness.

Beautiful patios can be glimpsed – often tantalisingly, through closed wrought-iron gates – in Córdoba's historic centre and other parts of town. They are at their prettiest in spring, and dozens of them open up for free public viewing until 10pm for two weeks in May during the very popular Fiesta de los Patios de Córdoba. The following are open to the public most of the year.

Palacio de Viana
A stunning Renaissance palace with 12 beautiful, plant-filled patios, the Viana Palace is a particular delight to visit in spring. Occupied by the aristocratic Marqueses de Viana until 1980, the large building is packed with art and antiques.

Asociación de Amigos de los Patios Cordobeses
This particularly lovely patio, dripping with bougainvillea and other plants, can be visited year-round. Its colourfulness depends on the season, but even if the blooms are disappointing you can still browse the several craft workshops within the patio.

Patios de San Basilio
You can visit this group of three interesting and well-tended Cordoban patios in the Alcázar Viejo area, about 400m southwest of the Mezquita, most of the year round.

Patio de los Naranjos (Mezquita)
This attractive courtyard, with its orange, palm and cypress trees and fountains, forms the entrance to the Mezquita. It was the site of ritual ablutions before prayer in the mosque. Its most impressive entrance is the Puerta del Perdón, a 14th-century Mudéjar archway next to the bell tower.

To read about:
White Villages of Andalucía see page 110
Horse Riding in Andalucía see page 148

Salamanca: The Golden City

CASTILLA Y LEÓN PEOPLE & CULTURE

Luminous when floodlit, the elegant central square of Salamanca, the Plaza Mayor, is possibly the most attractive in all of Spain. It is just one of many highlights in a city whose architectural splendour has few peers in the country. Salamanca is a university town, so student revelry also lights up the nights. It's this combination of grandeur and energy that makes so many people call Salamanca their favourite city in Spain.

Only when the last rays of afternoon sunshine clear the sandstone facade of Salamanca's Plaza Mayor does the most magnificent town square in Spain really come to life. Elderly couples shuffle along colonnaded walkways; children play tag and dribble melting ice cream over the paving slabs; students clatter away on their laptops in the cafes. Gazing sternly over the whole scene are the greatest minds and bravest souls in all of Spanish history: explorer Columbus, conquistador Cortés, writer Cervantes – their profiles etched into the stone arches. Inches above their heads, local residents lean on cast-iron balconies and study the square in expectation.

Home to Spain's oldest and most prestigious university, Salamanca has the double fortune of being quite possibly the nation's brainiest and most beautiful city. Biscuity-ochre towers rise over the city, sending long shadows creeping down alleyways along which students pedal to their lectures. Ancient faculties line cypress-shaded squares – their stones bearing Latin inscriptions from alumni who graduated centuries ago, some painted in bull's blood. Hogging the skyline are twin cathedrals that survived the 1755 earthquake which destroyed Lisbon, and still sport broken windows and cracked walls from the tremors, while south of the city is the wide, sluggish expanse of the Río Tormes, slipping beneath a Roman bridge on its way to the Portuguese Atlantic.

Gaining admission to Salamanca University has never been easy, nor has paying the tuition fees. Fortunately some especially bright students hit on a novel solution to this latter problem. On the stroke of nine each night, two groups wearing shiny shoes, tight trousers and colourful sashes shuffle into the square, armed with an assortment of accordions, double basses, mandolins, guitars and tankards of beer. Soon the far corners of Plaza Mayor are noisy with the twangs, claps, shouts and whoops of the *tunas*. Groups of troubadours like these have busked to pay their study fees since the 13th century, with each band linked to a particular university faculty.

Salamanca's traditions have endured through the many turbulent chapters of Spanish history. The university's most famous story concerns the poet Luis de León, snatched from a lecture by the Inquisition for having translated the 'Song of Solomon' into Spanish. The sardonic theologian returned to his class after five years in jail and resumed lecturing with the words, 'As I was saying yesterday...'

To read about:
The Land of Don Quixote see page 152
Segovia's Roman Aqueduct see page 158

White Villages of Andalucía

Discover a world of whitewashed homes tucked into green-cloaked country, along with crag-top castles, volatile frontier history, peaceful walks and mysterious mazelike streets on this mountain-flavoured drive that weaves together Andalucía's prettiest pueblos blancos *(white towns).*

Right **Setenil de las Bodegas**

Carmona

Crowning a low-rise Campiña hill, Carmona is like a living snapshot of Andalucian history. Its old town is a maze of centuries-old monuments, majestic Mudéjar and Christian palaces, churches and convents, and buzzy tapas bars – the perfect introduction to your white-towns tour.

Marvel over sights such as the splendidly over-the-top 15th- and 16th-century Iglesia Prioral de Santa María de la Asunción, its gorgeous columned Patio de los Naranjos sporting a Visigothic calendar. Exquisite Roman mosaics remain preserved inside the town hall, and on the southwestern fringe of town stands the eerily fascinating 1st- and 2nd-century Necrópolis Romana.

Arcos de la Frontera

Everything you've ever dreamed a *pueblo blanco* could be miraculously materialises in Arcos de la Frontera. A sea of red-tile-roofed, whitewashed houses tumbles down from a sheer-sided crag, atop which huddles a soporific old-town labyrinth full of historical mystery. Over two centuries between the Christian conquest of Seville (1248) and the final Muslim emirate, Granada (1492), Arcos and its 'on the frontier' companions straddled the unstable Christian–Moorish border.

The main attraction is Plaza del Cabildo for spectacular vistas over the Río Guadalete from its vertical-edged mirador (lookout). But the knockout view is the dramatic cliff-top panorama from the swanky adjacent *parador* (luxurious state-owned hotel) – best drunk in over a reinvigorating *café con leche* (milky coffee).

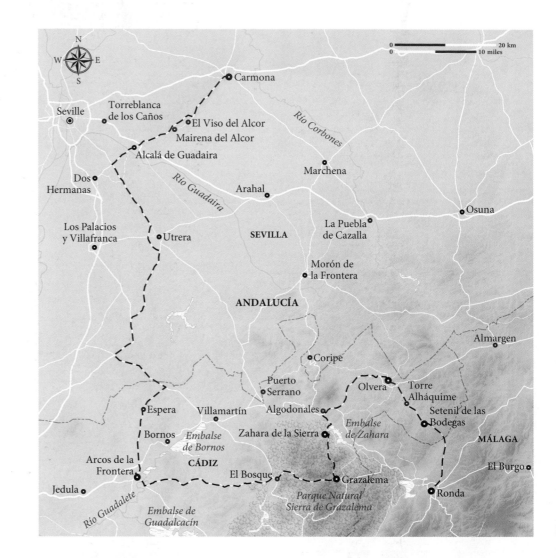

Grazalema

Craving some physical activity? Clinging to green-clad rocky slopes, rust-roofed Grazalema is an idyllic white mountain town, but it's also your best stopover for exploring the rugged, 534-sq-km Parque Natural Sierra de Grazalema. This is the rainiest spot in Spain, and all the more picturesque for it. Hike the El Calvario trail to a ruined chapel, or choose from numerous gorgeous Sierra walking paths starting near Grazalema.

Back in town, the Museo de Artesanía Textil reveals the age-old techniques behind Grazalema's famous wool blankets. The town is also an age-old producer of honey and cheeses; perfect for picnics.

Zahara de la Sierra

Rugged Zahara, strung around a vertiginous spur at the foot of the Grazalema mountains, overlooking the glittering turquoise Embalse de Zahara, hums with Moorish mystery. For more than 150 years in the 14th and 15th centuries, it stood on the old medieval frontier facing off against Christian Olvera, clearly visible in the distance. These days Zahara ticks all the classic white-town boxes and, with vistas framed by tall palms and hot-pink bougainvillea, its streets invite exploration.

In town, it's a steepish 10- to 15-minute climb to the 12th-century castle. It was under Christian rule from 1407, but in 1481 Abu al-Hasan of Granada recaptured it overnight, triggering a Christian backlash that ended in the definitive reconquest of all that remained of Moorish Spain.

Olvera

Dramatically topped by a Moorish-era castle, Olvera beckons from miles away

Above **Olvera**

across olive-covered country. Reconquered by Alfonso XI in 1327, this relatively untouristed town was a bandit refuge until the mid-19th century. Most people now come to Olvera to walk or cycle the Vía Verde de la Sierra, considered the finest of Andalucía's 23 *vías verdes* (hiking/cycling greenways made from disused railway lines).

As a white town par excellence, Olvera itself is well worth exploring. Climb past lime-washed walls and red roofs to the late 12th-century castle, the neoclassical church and the Museo de La Frontera y Los Castillos.

Setenil de las Bodegas

While most white towns sought protection atop lofty crags, the people of Setenil de las Bodegas did the opposite and burrowed into the dark caves beneath the steep cliffs of the Río Trejo. Clearly, the strategy worked: the Christian armies had to stage a 15-day siege to dislodge the Moors from their well-defended positions in 1484. Many of the town's original cave-houses remain to explore, some converted into tapas bars and restaurants, and Setenil is now an increasingly popular day trip from the Ronda and Grazalema areas.

Ronda

End your road trip on a literal high. Spectacularly carved in half by the 100m-wide Tajo gorge, rugged Ronda revels in mountain drama. It's Málaga's most striking white town, one of Spain's oldest settlements, and the (alleged) birthplace of bullfighting. Ronda's towering 18th-century Puente Nuevo straddles the gorge between the new town (north)

Above Arcos de la Frontera; Right **Ronda**

Sierra de Grazalema Walks

Garganta Verde Starting 3.5km south of Zahara de la Sierra (off the CA9104), this 2.5km (one hour) path meanders down into the precipitous Garganta Verde ('Green Throat') with huge griffon vultures whooshing past at eye level. It's one of the Sierra's most spectacular walks.

El Torreón Climb Cádiz province's highest peak (1654m) for unbeatable Gibraltar, Sierra Nevada and Morocco views. The 3km trail (2½ hours) begins 8km west of Grazalema on the A372.

El Pinsapar This 12km (six hour) walk winds past rare dark-green *pinsapos* (Spanish firs) to Benamahoma. It starts 2km uphill from Grazalema off the CA9104.

and old town (La Ciudad, south). Savour La Ciudad's ancient soul as you wander its walled, Islamic-era tangle of narrow streets, flavoured by fine Renaissance mansions and intriguing museums.

The Museo Lara hosts the impressive, eclectic private collection of Juan Antonio Lara Jurado. Across the chasm, Plaza de España and its grisly Spanish Civil War history were immortalised in Hemingway's *For Whom the Bell Tolls*.

To read about:
Alhambra: The Jewel of Granada see page 122
Aragón: The Villages Time Forgot see page 142

Olive Oil: A Taste of Jaén

ANDALUCÍA FOOD & DRINK

Where would Spain, and indeed the world, be without olive oil? Forget Italy and Greece – more olive oil is produced in Spain than anywhere else on the planet. There are over 100 million olive trees in Andalucía alone, and a remarkable 20% of the world's olive oil originates in Jaén province, which produces more olive oil than Greece. In fact, Jaén's 4500 sq km of olive trees constitute the world's largest artificial forest.

Southern Spain's olive groves were originally planted by the Romans, but the production of *az-zait* (the juice of the olive), from which the modern generic word for olive oil, aceite, is derived, was further developed by the Muslims.

The most common type of olive used for making olive oil is the full-flavoured and (sometimes) vaguely spicy *picual*, which dominates the olive groves of Jaén province and accounts for 50% of all Spanish olive production. It takes its name from its pointed *pico* (tip), and is considered ideal for olive oil due to its high proportion of vegetable fat, natural antioxidants and polyphenol; the latter ensures that the oil keeps well and maintains its essential qualities at a high cooking temperature.

Another important type of olive is the *hojiblanco*. Its oil, which keeps for less time and should be stored in a cool dark place, is said to have a taste and aroma reminiscent of fruits, grasses and nuts.

Olives Rule
You can't fail to notice that in the province of Jaén, the *olivo* (olive tree) rules. More than 60 million olive trees carpet a full 40% of the landscape, and the aroma of their oil perfumes memories of any visit. In an average year these trees yield about 500,000 tonnes of olive oil, meaning that Jaén produces 40% of Spain's production. Almost the whole population depends, directly or indirectly, on this one crop.

Olives are harvested from October until about February. They are taken straight to oil mills to be mashed into a pulp that is then pressed to extract the oil, and decanted to remove water. Oil that's good enough for consumption without being refined is sold as *aceite de oliva virgen* (virgin olive oil), and the best of that is *virgen extra*. Plain *aceite de oliva* – known in the trade as *lampante* (lamp oil) – is oil that has to be refined before it's fit for consumption. Oils are tested for chemical composition and taste in International Olive Council laboratories before they can be labelled virgin or extra virgin.

Technological Revolution
A technological revolution has changed the face of the olive-oil world since the late 20th century. On the way out, except in some smaller operations, are the traditional methods of harvesting (teams of people bashing the branches with poles), pulping (great conical stone rollers), pressing (squashing layers of pulp between esparto-grass mats) and decanting (four or five repeated processes taking eight or nine hours). Today's olives are shaken off the trees by tractor-driven vibrating machines; they are pulped mechanically; and centrifuge machines separate the liquids from the solids and do most of the decanting – all in a fraction of the time it used to take.

Tasting & Learning
Jaén is proud of its high-quality olive oil: many restaurants will offer you a few different types to try, soaked up with bread. Quality oil is sold in specialist shops and good groceries, and direct at some mills.

Oleícola San Francisco runs fascinating tours of a working oil mill near Baeza, which will teach you all you could want to know about the process of turning olives into oil, how the best oil is made and what distinguishes extra virgin from the rest.

Denominación de Origen
Olive-oil production is almost as complicated as that of wine, with a range of designations to indicate quality. The best olive oils are those classified as 'virgin' (which must meet 40 criteria for quality and purity) and 'extra virgin' (the best olive oil, with acidity levels no higher than 1%). Accredited olive-oil-producing regions receive the designation Denominación de Origen (DO, which indicates the unique geographic origins, production processes and quality of the product). DO regions in Andalucía include Baena and Priego de Córdoba in Córdoba, and Sierra de Segura and Sierra Mágina in Jaén.

At the end you get to taste a few varieties, and you'll probably emerge laden with a bottle or two of San Francisco's high-quality product.

The Centro de Interpretación Olivar y Aceite, Úbeda's olive-oil interpretation centre, explains all about the area's olive-oil history, and how the oil gets from the tree to your table. Here you will also get the chance to taste different oils, and to buy from a broad selection.

To read about:
Gazpacho: Summertime Soup see page 96
Cycling the Railways of Andalucía see page 192

Living History

Monuments of Art & Architecture

Spain's story is one of history's grand epics, and the landmarks left behind infuse every aspect of the Spanish experience.

The story begins with the remarkably sophisticated artworks of the ancients in the caves of Cantabria, a priceless record of an era otherwise lost to time. It progresses through ancient civilisations – Phoenicians, Greeks and Romans – who all sought to rule ancient Iberia (founded by the Phoenicians in 1104 BC, Cádiz is a candidate for the title of the continent's oldest city). Centuries later, armies, ideas and religions clashed upon the soil of Spain. From the 7th to the 15th centuries, Muslim Moors battled Christian kings, but the good guys inhabited both sides and medieval Spain was often a tolerant, enlightened place. These struggles for supremacy bequeathed to the country an extravagantly rich portfolio of buildings that is unmatched in Europe – cathedrals, pleasure palaces, castles, even entire cities of architectural treasures.

There is little need for museums to tell this story, although good museums abound. Grand monuments each tell their chapter of history – the Roman aqueduct in Segovia; Moorish splendour in Granada, Seville and Córdoba; cathedrals in Santiago de Compostela, León, Burgos or Toledo. But to truly inhabit the picaresque tales of Spain's past, all you have to do is climb high onto windswept fortress walls in the country's interior, or lose yourself in the tangle of alleyways and teahouses of Granada's Albayzín, and listen to Spain tell its story.

Alhambra: The Jewel of Granada

With the snow-dusted Sierra Nevada as a backdrop, this towering, hilltop Moorish citadel has been rendering visitors of one kind or another speechless for a millennium. The reason: its harmonious architectural balance between humankind and the natural environment. Fear not the dense crowds: the Alhambra is an essential pilgrimage.

ANDALUCÍA ARCHITECTURE

The origins of the Alhambra, whose name derives from the Arabic *al-qala'a al-hamra* (the Red Castle), are mired in mystery. The first references to construction in the area appear in the 9th century but it's thought that buildings may already have been standing since Roman times. In its current form, it largely dates to the 13th and 14th centuries when Granada's Nasrid rulers transformed it into a fortified palace complex. Following the 1492 Reconquista (Christian reconquest), its mosque was replaced by a church and the Habsburg emperor Charles V had a wing of palaces demolished to make space for the huge Renaissance building that still bears his name. Later, in the early 19th century, French Napoleonic forces destroyed part of the palace and attempted to blow up the entire site. Restoration work began in the mid-1800s and continues to this day.

Alcazaba

Occupying the western tip of the Alhambra are the martial remnants of the Alcazaba, the site's original 13th-century citadel. A winding staircase leads to the top of the Torre de la Vela (Watchtower) where you can enjoy sweeping views over Granada's rooftops.

Palacios Nazaríes

The Alhambra's stunning centrepiece, the palace complex known as the Palacios Nazaríes, was originally divided into three sections: the Mexuar, a chamber for administrative and public business; the Palacio de Comares, the emir's official and private residence; and the Palacio de los Leones, a private area for the royal family and harem.

From the Mexuar, a 14th-century hall where the emir would adjudicate citizens' appeals, you pass into the Patio del Cuarto Dorado, with the Cuarto Dorado (Golden Room) on the left. Of the four halls around the patio, the southern Sala de los Abencerrajes is the most impressive. Boasting a mesmerising octagonal stalactite ceiling, this is the legendary site of the murders of the noble Abencerraj family. The rusty stains in the fountain are said to be the victims' indelible blood.

On the patio's northern side is the richly decorated Sala de Dos Hermanas (Hall of Two Sisters), featuring a dizzying *muqarnas* (honeycomb-vaulted) dome with a central star and 5000 tiny cells, reminiscent of the constellations.

Generalife

The Generalife, the sultans' gorgeous summer estate, dates to the 14th century. A soothing ensemble of pathways, patios, pools, fountains, trees and, in season, flowers of every imaginable hue, it takes its name from the Arabic *jinan al-'arif*, meaning 'the overseer's gardens'.

To read about:
Castles & Cathedrals see page 138
Cycling the Railways of Andalucía see page 192

Moorish Legacy

Muslim rule left an indelible imprint upon Spain. It was through 800 years of Moorish rule that much of the learning of ancient Greece and Rome – picked up by the Arabs in the eastern Mediterranean – was transmitted to Christian Europe, where it would exert a profound influence on the Renaissance. The Islamic centuries left a deep imprint that still permeates Andalucian life, and a legacy of unique monuments: Granada's Alhambra, Córdoba's great Mezquita and Seville's Alcázar are windows into the splendours of the age and essential Andalucian cultural experiences.

Andalucía was under Muslim rule, wholly or partly, for nearly eight centuries from 711 to 1492 – a time span much longer than the five centuries that have passed since 1492. For much of those eight centuries Andalucía was the most cultured and economically advanced region in a Europe that for the most part was going through its 'Dark Ages'.

Arabs carried Islam through the Middle East and North Africa following the death of the Prophet Mohammed in 632. In 711 Tariq ibn Ziyad, the Muslim governor of Tangier, landed at Gibraltar with around 10,000 men, mostly indigenous North African Berbers. They decimated the army of the last Visigothic king, Roderic, probably near the Río Guadalete in Cádiz province, and Roderic is thought to have drowned as he fled.

Within a few years, the Muslims had taken over the whole Iberian Peninsula except for small areas in the Asturian mountains in the far north. The name given to the Muslim-ruled territories was Al-Andalus. From this comes the modern name of the region that was always the Islamic heartland on the peninsula – Andalucía.

In the centuries that followed, Moorish architecture incorporated trends from all over the Islamic world. The technique of intricately carved stucco detailing was developed in 9th-century Iraq, while *muqarnas* (honeycomb vaulting) arrived via Egypt in the 10th century. Square minarets, such as the Giralda in Seville (now a cathedral tower), came with the Almohad invasion from Morocco in the 12th century.

In the main cities, the Muslims built beautiful palaces, mosques and gardens, opened universities and established public bathhouses and bustling *zocos* (markets). The Moorish society of Al-Andalus was a mixed bag. The ruling class was composed of various Arab groups prone to factional friction. Below them was a larger group of Berbers, some of whom rebelled on numerous occasions. Jews and Christians had freedom of worship, but Christians had to pay a special tax, so most either converted to Islam or left for the Christian north. Christians living in Muslim territory were known as Mozarabs (*mozárabes* in Spanish); those who adopted Islam were muwallads *(muladíes)*. Before long, Arab, Berber and local blood merged, and many Spaniards today are partly descended from medieval Moors.

Tellingly, the conquering Christian armies of 1492 may have disposed of the emirs and government of Al-Andalus, but they didn't have the heart to flatten all of the Moors' most iconic buildings. While they knocked down some mosques and replaced them with churches, other mosques were simply repurposed for the new religion. Fortresses, palaces and mansions were often re-used and adapted as the centuries went by. As a result, Andalucía's architecture is a story of layers, hybrids and Christian–Moorish intermixing.

Today, 500 years since the fall of Granada, the impact of the Islamic centuries is never far from the surface. Thousands of buildings large and small are Moorish in origin (including the many churches that began life as mosques). The narrow street plans of many a Spanish town and village, especially in the south, date back to Moorish times. In the hearts of these towns (as in Granada's Albayzín), the intricate tangles of streets are redolent of North African medinas.

Left Courtyard of the Maidens, Alcázar

The Moors introduced many key ingredients into Spanish cooking, including rice and saffron, which come together in paella; almonds, used in countless Spanish desserts; eggplants and apricots, the former present in the popular tapa *berenjenas con miel de caña* (eggplants with molasses); and numerous spices, several of which combine in, among other dishes, the *pincho moruno* (spicy chicken kebab). The irrigated terrace systems created by the Moors to grow crops and vegetables remain a key source of the same foods today. The Spanish language also contains many common words of Arabic origin, including the names of some of those new crops – *naranja* (orange), *azúcar* (sugar) and *arroz* (rice). Flamenco, though brought to its modern form by Roma people in post-Moorish times, has clear Moorish roots.

The Islamic love of ornate, scented gardens with flowing or trickling water – hidden inner sanctums that safeguarded residents from prying eyes – can also be seen in patios, courtyards and the carefully manicured greenery that embellishes Andalucía's Moorish-influenced houses and palaces.

Mezquita (Córdoba)

It's impossible to overemphasise the beauty of Córdoba's great mosque, with its serene and spacious interior. One of the world's greatest works of Islamic architecture, the Mezquita hints, with all its lustrous decoration, at a refined age when Muslims, Jews and Christians lived side by side and enriched their city with a heady interaction of diverse, vibrant cultures.

The Mezquita's architectural uniqueness and importance lies in the fact that, structurally speaking, it was a

Above **Interior detail**, Alcázar; Right **Mezquita**

Hammams

Sitting somewhere between a Western spa and a Moroccan *hammam*, Andalucía's modern bath-houses possess enough old-fashioned elegance to satisfy a latter-day emir with a penchant for Moorish-era opulence. You can recline in candlelit subterranean bliss sipping mint tea, and experience the same kind of bathing ritual – successive immersions in cold, tepid and hot bathwater – that the Moors did.

revolutionary building for its time. Earlier major Islamic buildings such as the Dome of the Rock in Jerusalem and the Great Mosque in Damascus placed an emphasis on verticality, but the Mezquita was intended as a democratically horizontal and simple space, where the spirit could be free to roam and communicate easily with God.

Its most innovative features include some early horseshoe arches, an intricate *mihrab* (prayer niche indicating the direction of Mecca), and a veritable 'forest' of 856 columns, many of them recycled from Roman ruins. The sheer scale of the Mezquita reflects Córdoba's erstwhile power as the most cultured city in 10th-century Europe.

Alcázar (Seville)

A magnificent marriage of Christian and Mudéjar architecture, Seville's Unesco-listed palace complex is a breathtaking spectacle. The site, which was originally developed as a fort in 913, has been re-

**Far left Hammam
Al Ándalus Granada**;
Left Stucco wall,
Alhambra;
Right Aljafería

vamped many times over the 11 centuries of its existence, most spectacularly in the 14th century when King Pedro added the sumptuous Palacio de Don Pedro, the Alcázar's crown jewel. King Pedro, though at odds with many of his fellow Christians, had a long-standing alliance with the Muslim emir of Granada, Mohammed V, the man responsible for much of the decoration at the Alhambra. So when Pedro decided to build a new palace in the Alcázar in 1364, Mohammed sent many of his top artisans. Their work, drawing on the Islamic traditions of the Almohads and caliphal Córdoba, is a unique synthesis of Iberian Islamic art.

Aljafería (Zaragoza)
The Aljafería is Spain's finest Islamic-era edifice outside Andalucía. Built as a fortified palace for Zaragoza's Muslim rulers in the 11th century, it underwent various alterations after 1118 when Zaragoza passed into Christian hands. In the 1490s the Reyes Católicos (Catholic Monarchs), Fernando and Isabel, tacked on their own palace. From the 1590s the Aljafería was developed into more of a fortress than a palace. Twentieth-century restorations brought it back to life, and Aragón's regional parliament has been housed here since 1987.

To read about:
Córdoba's Patios in Bloom see page 106
Castles & Cathedrals see page 138

Ancient Extremadura

Exploring Extremadura is a journey into the heart of old Spain, from the country's finest Roman ruins to mysterious medieval cities and time-worn villages. Mérida, Cáceres and Trujillo rank among Spain's most beautifully preserved historical settlements. Extremeño hamlets have a timeless charm, from the remote northern hills to sacred eastern Guadalupe.

Right **Teatro Romano**, Mérida

Extremadura is one of Spain's least-visited corners, but that would surely change if only people knew what was here. This is a land where the stories of ancient civilisations, the golden age of Spanish exploration and untold medieval riches are written in stone, with magnificent old cities and villages strung out across a splendid terrain of rolling hills and big horizons. This journey traverses Spain's ancient past, from stirring Roman ruins to tight tangles of medieval old quarters and castles that evoke a picaresque past.

Mérida

Mérida, capital of Extremadura, is a marvellous place to begin your journey, home as it is to the most impressive set of Roman ruins in all Spain. The glittering jewels are the 1st-century-BC Teatro Romano, a classical theatre still used for performances during the summer Festival del Teatro Clásico, and the adjacent Museo Nacional de Arte Romano. But in Mérida such splendours are just the beginning. There's the 60-arch Puente Romano that spans the Río Guadiana, the Templo de Diana that rises improbably from the modern city centre, and the Alcazaba, a fortress that has been occupied through the ages by everyone from Visigoths and Romans to the Muslims of Al-Andalus.

Trujillo

The core of Trujillo is one of the best-preserved medieval towns in Spain. It begins in the Plaza Mayor, surrounded by towers and palaces, and continues up the hillside with a labyrinth of mansions, leafy courtyards, fruit gardens, churches and convents all enclosed within 900m of walls circling the upper town and dating back to the 16th century. At the top of the hill, Trujillo's impressive Alcazaba has 10th-century Islamic origins. Patrol the battlements for magnificent 360-degree sweeping views. Don't miss the less-visited western end of the upper old town, with its cobbles, palaces and flower-filled plazas. Whether bathed in the warm light of a summer sunset or shrouded in the mists of winter, Trujillo is a magical place.

Guadalupe

Centred on its palatial monastery, a treasure trove of art, architecture and history, the sparkling white village of Guadalupe is a hugely popular pilgrimage centre. The town's revered Real Monasterio de Santa María de Guadalupe is located, according to legend, on the spot where a shepherd found an effigy of the Virgin, hidden years earlier by Christians fleeing Muslim rule. The monastery now contains works attributed to El Greco, Goya, Zurbarán and even Michelangelo.

Granadilla

The ghost village of Granadilla is a beguiling reminder of how Extremadura's villages must have looked before modernisation. Founded by the Moors in the 9th century but abandoned in the 1960s when the nearby dam was built, Granadilla's traditional architecture has been painstakingly restored since the 1980s as part of a government educational project. Enter through the narrow Puerta de Villa, overlooked by the sturdy 15th-century castle, which you can climb for brilliant panoramas.

From the Puerta de Villa, the cobblestone Calle Mayor climbs up to delightfully rustic Plaza Mayor, surrounded by

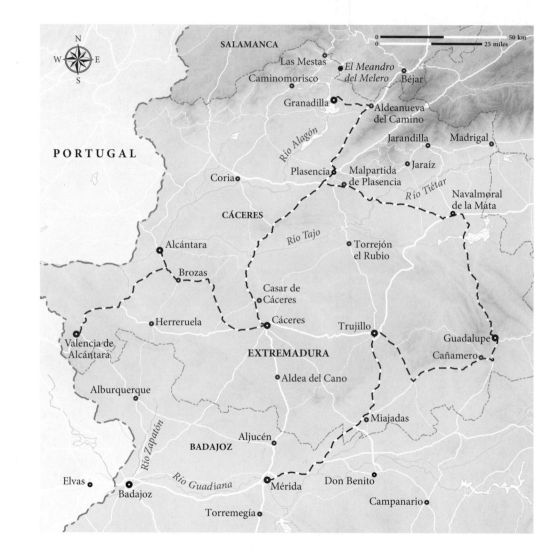

El Meandro del Melero

One of Extremadura's most beautiful geographical features, El Meandro del Melero is where the Río Alagón does an extraordinary loop, forming a near-perfect oxbow formation around a forested, teardrop-shaped island. It's at its best when the river is at full capacity, but even during a recent drought with little water it was still spectacular. The best views are from the Mirador de La Antigua.

vibrant buildings. On the right stands the beautiful Casa de las Conchas, its peach-coloured exterior studded with white ceramic shells. Don't miss a stroll along the top of the 1km-long Almohad walls, with evocative views of village, lake, eucalyptuses and pinewoods.

Cáceres

The old core of Cáceres, its Ciudad Monumental (Old Town), is truly extraordinary. Narrow cobbled streets twist and climb among ancient stone walls lined with palaces and mansions, while the skyline is decorated with turrets, spires, gargoyles and enormous storks' nests. Fuelled particularly by wealth brought from the Americas, the churches, palaces and towers are hugely impressive. Protected by defensive walls, it has survived almost intact from its 16th-century heyday and so much of the monumental beauty is clustered around three connected squares, the Plaza de Santa María, Plaza de San Jorge and Plaza de San Mateo. If

Far Left **Granadilla castle**;
Left **Architectural detail**, Real Monasterio de Santa María de Guadalupe;
Right **Alcántara**

you're lucky, a flamenco singer might be busking in one of the squares, adding to the magic. At dusk or after dark, when the crowds have gone, you'll feel like you've stepped back into the Middle Ages.

Alcántara
Out in Extremadura's wild, remote and rarely travelled west, Alcántara is best known for its magnificent Roman bridge. The bridge – 204m long, 61m high and much reinforced over the centuries – spans the Río Tajo below a huge dam. The town itself retains old walls, a ruined castle, several imposing mansions and the enormous Renaissance Convento de San Benito.

The highlights of the down-at-heel monastery, built in the 16th century to house the Orden de Alcántara, an order of Reconquista knights, include the Gothic cloister and the perfectly proportioned three-tier loggia.

Valencia de Alcántara
Not many travellers stop out here, 7km from the Portuguese border, and its well-preserved old centre is a curious labyrinth of whitewashed houses and mansions. One side of the old town is watched over by the ruins of a medieval castle and the 17th-century Iglesia de Rocamador. The surrounding countryside is known for its cork industry and some 50 ancient dolmens (stone circles of pre-historic monoliths).

To read about:
Aragón: The Villages Time Forgot see page 142
Segovia's Roman Aqueduct see page 158

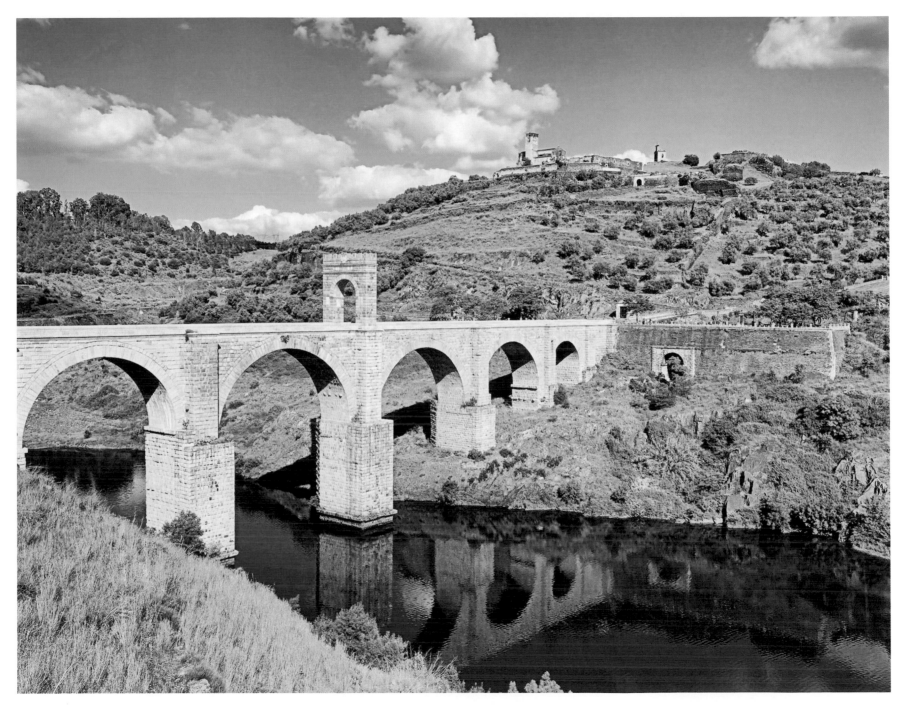

Montserrat's Mountain Monastery

CATALONIA LANDSCAPES & JOURNEYS

Montserrat is at the heart of Catalan identity for its mountain, monastery and natural park weaving among distinctive rock formations. Montserrat mountain is instantly recognisable, sculpted over millennia by wind and frost. Its turrets of rock, a coarse conglomerate of lime-stone and eroded fragments, extend like gnarled fingers from its 1236m-high bulk. More than halfway up the moun-tain lies the Benedictine Monestir de Montserrat, home to the Virgen de Montserrat, affectionately known as La Moreneta ('the Little Brown One' or 'the Black Madonna'), one of Spain's most revered icons.

Right **Monestir de Montserrat**

Walking Trails

Beyond the touristic hubbub surrounding Montserrat's monastery and basilica, there's tranquillity to be found in the web of walking trails across the mountain. Take the Funicular de Sant Joan for the first 250m uphill from the monastery; alternatively, it's a 45-minute walk along the road between the funicular's lower and upper stations. From the top, it's a 20-minute stroll to the Ermita de Sant Joan, with fine westward views. More exciting is the 7.5km (2½-hour) loop walk from the upper station, northwest to Montserrat's highest peak, Sant Jeroni (1236m), then back. The walk takes you across the upper part of the mountain, with a close-up experience of some of the rock pillars.

Colourful legends have sprung up around this holy place, including a folk tale that described jagged Montserrat mountain as sawn by angels to make a throne for the Virgin Mary. Founded in 1025, the monastery was wrecked by Napoleon's troops in 1811, then largely abandoned as a result of anticlerical legislation in the 1830s, and slowly rebuilt from 1858. Today, a community of 55 monks lives here. The monastery complex encompasses two blocks: on one side, the basilica and monastery buildings, and on the other, tourist and pilgrim facilities.

To read about:

The Catalan Identity see page 68
White Villages of Andalucía see page 110

Castles & Cathedrals Through the Ages

Catholicism stands at the heart of Spanish identity, and cathedrals, with their rich accumulation of architectural styles, form the monumental and spiritual centrepiece of many Spanish towns. The Middle Ages came alive with Romanesque cloisters and great Gothic cathedrals. It was also during this time that spectacular castles sprang up across the countryside, adding to one of Europe's most intriguing architectural stories.

SPAIN-WIDE ARCHITECTURE

As the tide turned against the Muslims, the Romanesque style was sweeping medieval Europe, taking root in Spain in part because it was the aesthetic opposite of Islamic fashions – the Catalan architect and art historian Josep Puig i Cadafalch posited that each Romanesque detail was a systematic riposte to an Islamic one. These buildings were spare, angular and heavy, inspired by the proportions of classical structures. Many Romanesque structures were not-so-subtle statements about the success of the Reconquista.

Romanesque structures had perfectly semicircular arches – none of the stylised horseshoe look that had come before. In churches, this was expressed in a semicylindrical apse (or, in many cases, triple apse), a shape previously found in Byzantine churches. Entrances supported stacks of concentric arches – the more eye-catching because they were often the only really decorative detail. Great examples of the style include the Iglesia de San Martín in Frómista, and Sant Climent de Taüll, one of many fine examples in the Catalan Pyrenees. Later, during the 12th century, Spanish architects began to modify these semicircles, edging towards the Gothic style, as they added pointed arches and ribbed vaults. The Monasterio de la Oliva in Navarra was among the first to show such features, and cathedrals in Ávila, Sigüenza and Tarragona all display transitional elements.

The trend elsewhere in Europe towards towering cathedrals made possible by the newfangled flying buttresses caught on in Spain by the 13th century, when the cathedrals at Burgos, León and Toledo were begun. Some changes were subtle, such as placing choir stalls in the centre of the nave, but one was unmissable: the towering, decorative *retablo* (altarpiece) that graced the new churches. Spanish Gothic architects also devised the star vault, a method of distributing weight with ribbed vaults projecting out from a central point.

Many great buildings were begun at the height of Romanesque fashion but not completed until long after the Gothic style had gained the upper hand. The cathedral in Burgos, for instance, was begun in 1221 as a relatively sober construction, but its 15th-century spires are a product of German-inspired late-Gothic imagination. Mudéjar influences also made themselves felt. Toledo boasts many gloriously original buildings with Gothic-Mudéjar flair, as do parts of Aragón.

The Catalan approach to the Gothic was more sober, bereft of pinnacles. Architects developed incredibly broad, unsupported vaults without the use of flying buttresses. Gothic is also scattered liberally across Andalucía, where the Reconquista arrived just when Gothic was coming into fashion.

Most of the innumerable castles scattered across the country also went up in Gothic times – an extraordinary example is the sumptuous castle at Coca, not far from

Segovia. In Barcelona, some marvellous civil Gothic architecture can be admired, including the once-mighty shipyards that are now home to the Museu Marítim.

At the end of the 15th century, the Isabelline Gothic look, inspired by the Catholic queen, reflected her fondness for Islamic exotica and heraldic imagery. It's on display in Toledo's San Juan de los Reyes and the Capilla Real in Granada, where Isabel and her husband, Fernando, are buried. The Gothic fascination lasted into the 16th century, when there was a revival of pure Gothic, perhaps best exemplified in the new cathedral in Salamanca, although the Segovia cathedral was about the last, and possibly most pure, Gothic structure raised in Spain.

Catedral de Santiago de Compostela

The grand heart of Santiago, the cathedral soars above the city in a splendid jumble of spires and sculpture. Built piecemeal over several centuries, its beauty is a mix of the original Romanesque structure (constructed between 1075 and 1211) and later Gothic and baroque flourishes. The cathedral's artistic high point is the Pórtico de la Gloria inside the west entrance, featuring 200 masterly Romanesque sculptures.

Catedral de Sevilla

Seville's immense cathedral is awe-inspiring in its scale and majesty. The world's largest Gothic cathedral, it was built between 1434 and 1517 over the remains of what had previously been the city's main mosque.

Above Catedral de Santiago de Compostela;
Right Retablo Mayor (main altarpiece), Catedral de Sevilla

The history of the cathedral goes back to the 15th century but the history of Christian worship on the site dates to the mid-13th century. In 1248, the Castilian king Fernando III captured Seville from its Almohad rulers and transformed their great 12th-century mosque into a church. Some 153 years later, in 1401, the city's ecclesiastical authorities decided to replace the former mosque, which had been damaged by an earthquake in 1356, with a spectacular new cathedral: 'Let's construct a church so large future generations will think we were mad', they quipped (or so legend has it). The result is the staggering cathedral you see today, officially known as the Catedral de Santa María de la Sede.

Alcázar de Segovia

Rapunzel towers, turrets topped with slate witches' hats and a deep moat at its base make the Alcázar a prototype fairy-tale castle – so much so that its design inspired Walt Disney's vision. Fortified since Roman days, the site takes its name from the Arabic *al-qasr* (fortress). It was rebuilt in the 13th and 14th centuries, but the whole lot burned down in 1862. What's there today is an evocative, over-the-top reconstruction of the original.

To read about:

Architecture of the Imagination see page 164
The Genius of Gaudí see page 244

Aragón:
The Villages
Time Forgot

ARAGÓN **LANDSCAPES & JOURNEYS**

Amid the clamour of modern Spain, a world away from the Spanish stereotype of sun, sand and sangría, the stone-built **pueblos** *(villages) of Aragón move to a different pace. These picturesque medieval settlements dot the serrated landscape from hilltop to sweeping ridge, capturing the spirit of Spain's epic historical story and landscapes.*

Right **Albarracín**

It was the ancient kingdom of Aragón that, together with Castilla, gave power and prestige to the Reconquista, forcefully confirming Spain's Christian identity in the late 15th century. In 1452 the north-western village of Sos del Rey Católico saw the birth of Fernando II, future king and the male half of one of history's most ruthless double acts. The Reyes Católicos (Catholic Monarchs) – Fernando II and Isabel I of Castilla – swept all before them until their armies brought an end to seven centuries of often-enlightened Muslim rule on the Iberian Peninsula.

The village where Fernando II's life began possesses few clues as to the significance of what would follow, though it is now a symbol for the traditional heartland of Spanish heritage. Draped along a ridgeline from where it surveys the surrounding plains, Sos del Rey Católico at once resembles a fortress and a Tuscan hill town bathed in honey-coloured stone. Its quiet byways rise steeply from the valley floor, snaking along the contours of its narrow perch and rising to a summit where castle and church stand sentinel, like icons of Ferdinand II's battle to secure Catholic supremacy.

Aside from its sweeping history, Aragón is dominated by a geography that is almost continental in its variety. In the far north, valleys, deep and verdant, cut far into the Pyrenees, shelter forgotten streams and terracotta-roofed hamlets, then rise in steep, forested hillsides to some of Europe's most shapely peaks. Inaccessible for much of the year, these villages – among them Torla, Hecho and Ansó – are sturdy refuges at the mercy of the capricious Pyrenean climate.

Where the mountains' foothills descend away to the south, Aínsa, like Sos del Rey Católico, colonised a hilltop in medieval times and has scarcely changed in the centuries since. Cobbled together in uneven stone, Aínsa has a colonnaded public square, fine views north towards distant peaks and just two 'streets' that rise and fall in subtle shades of multi-coloured stone.

In the hills before Aragón levels out, Alquézar, a pyramid-shaped village, is one of the canyoning capitals of Europe, while the isolated backcountry region of El Maestrazgo in Teruel is truly one of Spain's most delightfully forgotten corners. Where the horizonless *meseta* (high plateau) of central Spain takes hold, Fuendetodos (the birthplace of Goya in 1746) and Daroca (encircled by hilltop castle ramparts) serve as reminders that Aragón has always played its part in the onward march of Spanish history.

But in Aragón's deep south lies a village that could justly claim to be the prettiest in Spain. Albarracín has the quality of a quiet and intimate fairy tale. Once the capital of an 11th-century Islamic state, later an independent Christian kingdom, Albarracín is an enchanted blend of earthy red, pink and terracotta set against dark stone and bouldered hillsides. There is something timeless about this place; never more so than when the sun dips behind the castle ramparts and envelops the village in a silence broken only by soft footfalls on cobblestones.

To read about:

The Mountains of Picos de Europa see page 98
Montserrat's Monastery see page 136

What's Cooking in Aragón?

The kitchens and tables of Aragón are dominated by meat, which may come in inventive combinations with other ingredients in numerous gastro establishments, or in good old-fashioned grilled, roast or stewed form in more traditional restaurants.

The region's cold, harsh winds create the ideal conditions for curing *jamón* (ham); some of the best comes from the Teruel area, which has its own DO (Denominación de Origen; quality-certified producing region). Hearty *ternasco* (suckling lamb) is generally served roasted or as ribs with potatoes. With France just up the road, it's no surprise, perhaps, that *caracoles* (snails) are another Aragonese speciality.

Aragón's local cheeses, 130 varieties of them, should be tried wherever you go – those of Albarracín, Tronchón and Benasque are among the most highly rated. Alongside these dairy-based delights, vegetarians should also seek out *alubias pochas* (a tasty white-bean stew with peppers, tomatoes and onion).

The Aragonese love their baked goods too: anywhere from Zaragoza northwards, look out for *trenza de Almudévar,* a long, bread-like cake made from flour, egg yolks, butter, almonds, walnuts and raisins, with its strands woven together like plaits (*trenzas*).

Top *Pochas con almejas* (white-bean stew with clams); Bottom Alquézar

Baby-Jumping Festival

Surely there's no festival quite as strange as the baby-jumping festival of Castrillo de Murcia, a small village west of Burgos. Every year since 1620, this tiny village of around 250 inhabitants has marked the feast of Corpus Cristi by lining up the babies of the village on a mattress, while grown men dressed as 'El Colacho', a figure representing the devil, leap over up to six supine and, it must be said, somewhat bewildered babies at a time. Like most Spanish rites, it does have a purpose – the ritual is thought to ward off the devil. Fear not though, no baby has been injured in the recorded history of the fiesta.

To read about:

On the Trail: Horse Riding in Andalucía

ANDALUCÍA ADVENTURE

From Don Quixote to El Cid, Spain is a country with a special affinity for life in the saddle, and Andalucía is steeped in equestrian tradition. Since Moorish times, paths have linked the limestone sierras and frontier villages of the region, winding through cork forests, olive groves and, in springtime, pastures vivid with irises. Among the most atmospheric ways to meander these ancient caminos are on sure-footed local horses or walking alongside mules carrying wine, chorizo and traditional garbanzo stew for a picnic.

Andalucía is the chief breeding ground of the elegant and internationally esteemed Spanish thoroughbred horse, also known as the Cartujano or Andalucian. Countless good riding tracks crisscross Andalucía's marvellous landscapes, and many *picaderos* (stables) are ready to take you on a guided ride, be it for an hour or a week. Many of the mounts are Andalucians or Andalucian-Arab crosses – medium-sized, intelligent, good in traffic and, as a rule, easy to handle and sure-footed.

The provinces of Sevilla and Cádiz have perhaps the highest horse populations and concentrations of stables, but there are riding opportunities throughout the region. Among the many highlight experiences are trail rides in the Alpujarras and Sierra Nevada, and beach and dune riding just out of Tarifa.

The hub of Andalucía's horse culture is Jerez de la Frontera (Cádiz), home of the famous Feria del Caballo (Jerez Horse Fair). It takes place every May and celebrates flamenco, sherry and, above all, the region's much-treasured horses. Colourful parades of horses pass through the Parque González Hontoria fairgrounds in the town's north, the aristocratic-looking male riders decked out in flat-topped hats, frilly white shirts, black trousers and leather chaps, their female *crupera* (sideways pillion) partners in long, frilly dresses. The fair makes a tremendous end or beginning to a few days of riding through the baked Andalucian mountains.

To read about:
The Land of Don Quixote see page 152
Hiking Las Alpujarras see page 222

Granada's Literary Legacy

GRANADA CULTURE

Intellectual debate has long flourished in Granada's bars, cafes and teterías (tea-houses). It's a tradition that harks back to the early 1920s, when a group of poets, writers and musicians came together in a tertulia (a Spanish artistic/literary gathering) known as El Rinconcillo in the Café Alameda. Now, these Moorish-style teterías, carrying a whiff of Fez, Marrakesh or even Cairo in their ornate interiors, have been revived in Granada as a result both of North African migration and a local interest in the Moorish side of their heritage.

Right **Tetería**, Granada

The dimly lit, cushion-filled, fit-for-a-sultan *teterías* were the venue of choice for El Rinconcillo gatherings. Regularly holding court was Federico García Lorca, who had returned to Granada in 1921 after a period studying in Madrid, and classical composer Manuel de Falla, who had moved to the city from Cádiz the previous year. They were joined by the likes of classical guitarist Andrés Segovia, painter Ismael González de la Serna, poet Miguel Pizarro, Lorca's brother Francisco and many others.

Fascinated by flamenco and inspired by the baroque poetry of Luis de Góngora, El Rinconcillo wanted to celebrate the authenticity of Andalucian culture while also vanquishing the overly picturesque vision of Spain expounded by outsiders. In 1922 the group was instrumental in organising the Concurso de Cante Jondo, a flamenco-singing competition staged in the Alhambra that aimed to save the art from over-commercialisation. Five years later they reappeared at an event organised by the Ateneo de Sevilla to celebrate the 300th anniversary of Góngora's death, which was the first unofficial gathering of what later became known as the Generación del '27 (an influential group of Spanish writers and artists that included Salvador Dalí and Luis Buñuel).

Granada still exudes an edgy literary air in its diverse drinking establishments, although the Café Alameda is no longer in business. Its former digs are now occupied by the Restaurante Chikito, which in February 2015 placed a statue of El Rinconcillo's most famous member, Lorca, in its front bar, in the very corner where he and his compatriots once met, drank and sought to reinvent Spanish culture.

Granada's Best Teahouses

Granada's *teterías* have proliferated in recent years, but there's still something invitingly exotic about their dark atmospheric interiors, stuffed with lace veils, stucco and low, cushioned seats. Most offer a long list of aromatic teas and infusions, along with a selection of sticky Arabic sweets. Many still permit their customers to puff on *cachimbas* (hookah pipes).

Abaco Té Minimalist interiors, Alhambra views and a long list of teas and medicinal infusions.

Tetería Nazarí Treat yourself to a mint and cinnamon tea accompanied by a sweet Moroccan pastry.

Tetería Dar Ziryab *Arabian Nights*–style setting for a herbal tea and chat over a *cachimba*.

Tetería Kasbah The biggest and busiest of the teahouses on the Calle Calderería Nueva *tetería* strip.

To read about:

Alhambra: The Jewel of Granada see page 122
Moorish Legacy see page 124

The Land of Don Quixote

Few literary landscapes have come to define an actual terrain quite like the La Mancha portrayed in Miguel de Cervantes' 17th-century novel El ingenious hidalgo Don Quijote de la Mancha, *better known in Spain as* El Quijote.

Of all the heroes of the Spanish-speaking world – from footballers to bullfighters, painters to kings – one man in particular stands out. His face grins at you on bank notes; his silhouette appears on postcards; his story has been told in ballet, opera, film, a Broadway musical, a Picasso painting and even a Coldplay song. And rather uniquely among national heroes, he is revered for being useless. This man is the great writer Miguel de Cervantes' comic creation Don Quixote, and his homeland is Castilla-La Mancha. It is a landscape in widescreen mode – big skies and arrow-straight roads, a patchwork of scrubby fields extending to the horizon. Every so often crumbling castles appear, indistinct on hazy hilltops. It is a place where temperatures are high, mirages are many, and inhabitants are few.

In the midst of this barren landscape, the market town of Consuegra holds an annual medieval festival where the tales of Don Quixote come to life. For much of the year it is a sleepy place, where old couples perch on windowsills watching farmyard traffic rumble past. Every August, however, its citizens engage in a weekend-long binge of mead glugging and pork roasting in the main square, plus some energetic battle re-enacting in a medieval castle, which rises regally over the town. Minibuses full of archers shuttle about the streets, Moorish encampments are pegged beside the football pitch and processions of monks walk solemnly beneath the tourist information office. Consuegra's most famous chivalric hero was, of course, Don Quixote – for it was here, some say, that he charged on horseback, lance in hand, at his most fearsome enemy – which was not in fact a many-armed monster, but a windmill.

Fighting a windmill, and losing, is a defining moment in European literature and encapsulates the story of Don Quixote: a daydreamer who chose to live in a make-believe world of heroic adventures rather than humdrum real life. To some readers of *Don Quixote,* the hero is a blundering lunatic – but to others it is he who is sane, and the rest of the world that is crazy. And, just like the Don, the inhabitants of Consuegra have decided for one weekend a year to play at being lords, ladies, archers and knights – to briefly inhabit their own world of make-believe.

Staying for the Knight
There is little consensus as to where Don Quixote went next, and there are as many *rutas de Don Quijote* (Don Quixote routes) as there are La Mancha towns eager to claim an impeccable Cervantes pedigree. In fact, few towns are actually mentioned by name in the book.

One that does appear is the now-unremarkable town of Puerto Lápice, southeast of Toledo. It was here that Don Quixote stayed in an inn that he mistook for a castle and, after keeping watch over it all night, convinced the innkeeper to knight him. El Toboso, northeast of Alcázar de San Juan, also appears in the book as the home of Dulcinea, the platonic love of Quixote. Nowadays you'll find in El Toboso the 16th-century Casa-Museo de Dulcinea, as well as the obligatory Don Quixote statue and a library with more than 300 editions of the book in various languages.

Windmills
Don Quixote may have spent much of his quest tilting at windmills (*molinos de viento*), but nowhere in the book is the exact location of these 'monstrous giants', against whom honourable battles must be fought, revealed. A great many of the whitewashed towers still stand sentinel on rocky bluffs overlooking the plains of La Mancha – some preserved as museums, but most abandoned, their sails and cogs jammed solid and their roof spaces home only to nesting birds. They were spinning long before Cervantes published his novel in the early 1600s, and have forever been an icon of the region.

The finest windmills are arguably the nine of Consuegra, strung out along a ridgeline that rises from the pancake-flat plains, and clearly visible from far away. Mota del Cuervo, northeast of Alcázar de San Juan, also has some seven candidates, but Campo de Criptana is Consuegra's main rival. Only 10 of Campo de Criptana's original 32 windmills remain, but they sit dramatically above the town. Local legend also maintains that Cervantes was baptised in the town's Iglesia de Santa Maria.

To read about:
The Swords of Toledo see page 160
The Bullfighting Debate see page 188

Right Don Quixote de la Mancha and Sancho Panza sculptures by Lorenzo Coullaut-Valera

Cantabria's Prehistoric Cave Art

Cantabria's fissured limestone landscape served for millennia as a refuge for Palaeolithic people, who left behind some of the world's most remarkable prehistoric art. Ten different caves in Cantabria have been enshrined as Unesco World Heritage sites for their vividly rendered images of aurochs (an extinct cattle species), deer, bison, horses and other creatures, along with hand prints and geometric symbols such as the 40,000-year-old red disks at Cueva de El Castillo – widely recognised as Europe's most ancient cave paintings.

Cantabria stands out both for its multiplicity of sites and the intimacy of the experience. Several Cantabrian caves – such as the exquisite Cueva de Covalanas – limit group sizes to eight people or fewer. In a group this small, coming face to face with the lantern-lit 20,000-year-old image of a fleeing stag, traced in red pigment by the fingers of an unknown ancient hand, is a profound experience. Even at world-famous Altamira – where public visits are normally restricted to an impressive replica called the Neocueva – five lucky souls are chosen by lottery each Friday to tour the original cave. Whether you see the original or the copy, Altamira's richly pigmented representations of animals with arched backs and bent legs following the cave ceiling's natural contours are one of Cantabria's essential experiences.

Altamira

The cave was found by an amateur archaeologist, Marcelino Sanz de Sautuola, and his daughter Maria in 1879, after a landslide exposed an opening. The discovery caused a stir – even the king of Spain went to take a look. But the excitement was short-lived, with some claiming Sautuola had painted the images himself. When other caves started to be discovered across Europe, Sautuola's name was cleared. Some of the paintings have been dated at more than 35,000 years old, making them among the oldest in the world.

Cueva de Covalanas

In 2008, 17 Palaeolithic art caves across northern Spain were added to the Unesco World Heritage List, including Cantabria's Cueva de Covalanas, whose intricately designed deer depictions are true artistic masterpieces.

Discovered in 1903, the cave is home to several breathtakingly beautiful red-hued paintings dating to around 20,000 BC.

Cueva de El Castillo

The vast underground passageways of Puente Viesgo's Cueva de El Castillo are decorated with some 275 images, including deer, bison, horses, goats, aurochs and a rare mammoth, as well as hand prints and other symbols. In 2012 a red symbol here was named the oldest cave art in the world, though it lost this title in 2014 to cave paintings on the Indonesian island of Sulawesi.

To read about:
Ancient Extremadura see page 130
Sunset at Templo de Debod see page 274

Left Cave paintings of bison, Altamira

Segovia's Roman Aqueduct

That such a stunning monument to Roman grandeur has survived in the heart of a modern city is a miracle. Totally incongruous, Segovia's aqueduct rises from the streetscape like an Escher-esque mirage, repeating on and on seemingly ad infinitum. Erected here by the Romans in the 1st century AD, its 163 arches and neck-craning high point 28m above town will bowl you over.

The Devil's Work

Although no one really doubts that the Romans built the aqueduct, a local legend attributes the architectural marvel to the sulphur-tinged efforts of Old Nick himself. The story goes that two millennia ago a young girl, tired of carrying water from the well, vowed to sell her soul to the devil in return for an easier solution. The obliging Lucifer worked through the night, while the girl recanted and prayed to God for forgiveness. So, God sent the sun into the sky earlier than usual, catching the devil unawares with only a single stone lacking to complete the structure. The girl's soul was saved, but it seems that she got her wish anyway.

Unesco World Heritage–listed Segovia's most recognisable symbol is El Acueducto, an 894m-long engineering wonder that looks like an enormous comb plunged into the city. The Romans built the aqueduct with not a drop of mortar to hold its more than 20,000 uneven granite blocks together. It was originally part of a complex system of aqueducts and underground canals that brought water to Segovia from the mountains more than 15km away.

To get *the* screensaver snap of Segovia, head north out of town, towards Cuéllar, for around 2km. The view of the city unfolds in all its fairy-tale magic, with the aqueduct taking a deserved starring role.

To read about:
Legend & Luxury: Stay in a Parador see page 92
Baby-Jumping Festival see page 146

Nerves of Steel: The Swords of Toledo

CASTILLA-LA MANCHA ARTS & CRAFTS

Among the ramparts of the World Heritage–listed town of Toledo lies a traditional sword-making and steel-working centre that's been going strong since 500 BC. It was between the 15th and 17th centuries that its sword makers were at the peak of their skills and when Toledo's swords – famed for the strength of their steel – were regarded as the best in Europe.

Approaching Toledo by road today, the city reveals itself slowly from out of the heat haze. First and foremost comes the spire of the town's 13th-century cathedral, soaring unchallenged in a cloudless sky. Then follow the turrets of the fortresses and the towers of lesser churches, jostling for prominence below. Finally, the rest of the city barges into view: an exquisite muddle of pastel-coloured villas, colourful flower boxes and higgledy-piggledy rooftops, cascading down a hillside by a long, languorous bend in the Río Tajo.

Toledo's golden age came in the Middle Ages when it was known as the 'city of three cultures': a time when Christians, Jews and Muslims lived together in peace and harmony, their hometown renowned for academia and philosophy. Wandering around Toledo in the 21st century, surrounded by the ghosts of its mosques, churches and synagogues, it's still possible to imagine that a citizen might in one morning have heard the clanging of church bells, the muttered prayers of a rabbi and a muezzin's call echoing down from the minarets.

In fact you can still visit the humble Mezquita del Cristo de la Luz with its silent, shadowy prayer hall – the last surviving Moorish mosque of 10 that once dotted the city, while not so far away is the Sinagoga del Transito, a whitewashed synagogue with swooping horseshoe arches beyond a leafy courtyard, once one of 10 synagogues in Toledo's former *judería* (Jewish quarter). And within the cacophony of the Middle Ages you would have surely heard the clanking of blacksmiths as they made Toledo's most famous export.

For the past 150 years, the Zamorano family have kept this tradition alive as the last local dynasty of swordsmiths in the city, making swords for every occasion.

Shuffling among anvils and biscuit tins full of bolts in the sooty workshop, which has been declared to be of special artisan interest by the regional government of Castilla-La Mancha, you can spot blades used in theatrical productions, ceremonial swords and replica swords of the kind the conquistadors used to threaten Incas and take the Americas. They are still manufactured following the medieval Toledo process – fired in a forge and bashed into shape manually.

If the workshop is not too busy you might be able to visit it and watch the products being made, and perhaps, following in the tradition of the medieval knights who cantered across Europe to shop for Toledo swords, pick up a souvenir for yourself.

To read about:
Ancient Extremadura see page 130
Handmade in Madrid see page 270

Modernity

Design, Style & Innovation in Spanish Life

Having one foot planted in a fascinating past hasn't stopped Spain from rushing headlong into the future: Spain today is a mosaic of innovative architecture, inventive gastronomy, avant-garde art and the creative spirit released after the Franco years.

When military dictator Francisco Franco died in 1975 after four long decades of rule, Spain exploded into the modern world with all the pent-up energy of an ex-convent schoolgirl. It wasn't that the country hadn't once been good at embracing the new – most Spanish artists had been ahead of their time, the epitome being Pablo Picasso and his painting *Guernica*. Instead, the country had merely stood still culturally for much of the Franco era. Making up for lost time, Spaniards embraced democracy with sudden zeal as well as an anything-goes hedonism. There was more to it than just having a good time. Accompanying the *very* long nights was an outpouring of creativity that continues to ripple through every aspect of Spanish culture and society.

Liberated from the strictures of the grey recent past, fashion designers brought colour and bold designs to the catwalk and the high street. Spanish cinema, too, led by the original and enduring Pedro Almodóvar, burst into life, fuelling an industry that now counts Oscar-winning actors and directors among its number as well as a stunningly rich catalogue of recent films. Architecture has also played its part, with the world's most creative architectural brains contributing to a remarkable flourishing of new icons – Bilbao's Guggenheim, shimmering in rippling titanium shields, is merely the best known of many. And the country has popular culture covered as well – Spain has proved to be an attractive setting for well-known TV shows, most notably *Game of Thrones*.

Architecture of the Imagination

After the sober, restrictive Franco years, Spain has made up for lost time and, particularly since the 1990s, the unifying theme in architecture appears to be that anything goes. With creations of such daring popping up all over the country, it's becoming clear that Spain's future will be every bit as original as its past.

Modernity / 164

Right Metropol Parasol, Seville

Far left **Gas Natural Building**, Barcelona; **Left Atocha railway station**, Madrid; **Right Ciudad de las Artes y las Ciencias**, Valencia

Local heroes include Santiago Calatrava, who built his reputation with swooping, bone-white bridges. In 1996 he designed the futuristic Ciudad de las Artes y las Ciencias complex in Valencia. In 2000 he also built the Sondika Airport, in Bilbao, which has been nicknamed La Paloma (the Dove) for the winglike arc of its aluminium skin.

Catalan Enric Miralles had a short career, dying of a brain tumour in 2000 at the age of 45, but his Mercat de Santa Caterina in Barcelona shows brilliant colour and inventive use of arches. His Gas Natural Building, also in Barcelona, is a poetic skyscraper that juts both vertically and horizontally.

In 1996 Rafael Moneo won the Pritzker Prize, the greatest international honour for living architects, largely for his long-term contributions to Madrid's cityscape, such as the revamping of the Atocha railway station. His Kursaal Palace in San Sebastián is eye-catching – still staunchly functional, but shining, like two giant stones swept up from the sea.

It's perhaps this openness – even hunger – for outside creativity that marks the country's built environment today. Norman Foster designed the metro system in Bilbao, completed in 1995; the transparent, wormlike staircase shelters have come to be called fosteritos. But it was Frank Gehry's 1998 Museo Guggenheim Bilbao in the same city that really sparked the quirky-building fever. Now the list of contemporary landmarks includes Jean Nouvel's spangly, gherkin-shaped Torre Glòries in Barcelona; Richard Rogers' dreamy, wavy Terminal 4 at Madrid's Barajas airport; and Jürgen Mayer's Metropol Parasol in Seville.

To read about:
Guggenheim: The Bilbao Effect see page 168
The Genius of Gaudí see page 244

Guggenheim: The Bilbao Effect

Bilbao's shimmering titanium Museo Guggenheim Bilbao is one of modern architecture's most iconic buildings. The museum almost single-handedly lifted Bilbao out of its post-industrial depression and into the 21st century, boosting the city's inspired regeneration, stimulating further development and changing the face of regional tourism. For many travellers, this extraordinary building is the primary reason for visiting Bilbao.

For most, it's the architecture itself that is the real star of the Guggenheim show. Designed by Frank Gehry, the museum's flowing canopies, promontories, ship-like shapes, towers and flying fins are irresistible. Allow plenty of time to walk around the exterior, observing how the patterns and colours change with the light. Heading inside, the interior is purposefully vast. The cathedral-like atrium is more than 45m high, with light pouring in through the glass cliffs.

Gehry designed the museum with historical and geographical contexts in mind. The site was an industrial wasteland, part of Bilbao's wretched and decaying warehouse district on the banks of the Ría del Nervión. The gleaming titanium tiles that sheathe most of the building like giant herring scales are said to have been inspired by the architect's childhood fascination with fish.

Other artists have added their touch as well. Lying between the glass buttresses of the central atrium and the Ría del Nervión is a simple pool of water that emits mist in an installation by Fujiko Nakaya. Near the riverbank is Louise Bourgeois' *Maman,* a skeletal spider-like canopy said to symbolise a protective embrace. In the open area west of the museum, the child-favourite fountain sculpture randomly fires off jets of water. Jeff Koons' kitsch whimsy *Puppy,* a 12m-tall highland terrier made up of thousands of begonias, is on the city side of the museum. Bilbao has hung on to 'El Poop', who was only supposed to be a passing attraction as part of a world tour.

To read about:

Master of Illusion: Salvador Dalí

One of the 20th century's most recognisable icons, Salvador Dalí (1904–89) could have had the term 'larger than life' invented for him. He then would probably have decorated it with pink pineapples. Although he started off dabbling in cubism, Dalí became more readily identified with the surrealists. His 'hand-painted dream photographs', as he called them, are virtuoso executions brimming with fine detail and nightmare images dragged up from a feverish and Freud-fed imagination.

CATALONIA ART

A Master is Born

Born in Figueres, Dalí turned his hand to everything from film-making to painting to architecture to literature to jewellery making. His surrealist trajectory through the often-serious landscape of 20th-century Spain brought him into contact and collaboration with figures such as Pablo Picasso, Luis Buñuel, Federico García Lorca and (controversially) Franco. A raft of foreign celebrities flocked to be seen in his extravagant company.

Self-consciously eccentric and a constant source of memorable soundbites, Dalí was nevertheless in some ways a conservative figure and a devout Catholic. A 1929 visit to Cadaqués by French poet Paul Éluard and his Russian wife, Gala, caused an earthquake in Dalí's life: he ran off to Paris with Gala (who became his lifelong obsession and, later, his wife) and joined the surrealist movement. His long relationship with Gala provided the stable foundation that his whirligig life revolved around.

The celebrity, the extraordinarily prolific output and, let's face it, the comedy moustache tend to pull focus from the fact that Dalí was an artist of the highest calibre. In his paintings, Dalí's surrealism is often far more profound than it seems at first glance. The floppy clocks of his most famous work, *The Persistence of Memory,* are interpreted by some as a reference to the flexibility of time proposed by Einstein. His *Christ of St John of the Cross* combines expert composition, symbol-laden Renaissance-style imagery and a nostalgic, almost elegiac view of the Catalan coast that he so loved.

The Dalí Triangle

Northeastern Catalonia's so-called Dalí Triangle encompasses the spectacularly out-of-this-world Teatre-Museu Dalí in Figueres, the artist's eclectic home at Port Lligat's Casa Museu Dalí near Cadaqués, and the conversely less flamboyant Castell de Púbol, northeast of Girona.

Teatre-Museu Dalí

No one but Salvador Dalí pops into your head when you lay eyes on this red castle-like building, topped with giant eggs and stylised Oscar-like statues and studded with plaster-covered croissants. An entirely appropriate final resting place for the master of surrealism, it has assured his immortality. Exhibits range from enormous, impossible-to-miss installations – like *Taxi plujós* (Rainy Taxi), an early Cadillac surmounted by statues – to the more discreet, including a tiny, mysterious room with a mirrored flamingo.

Between 1961 and 1974, Dalí converted Figueres' former municipal theatre, destroyed by a fire in 1939 at the end of the civil war, into the Teatre-Museu Dalí. It's full of illusions, tricks and the utterly unexpected, and contains a substantial portion of Dalí's life's work, though you won't find his most famous pieces here (they're scattered around the world).

Even outside, the building aims to surprise, from its entrance watched over by medieval suits of armour balancing baguettes on their heads, to bizarre sculptures outside the entrance on Plaça de Gala i Salvador Dalí, to the pink walls along Pujada al Castell and Carrer Canigó. The Torre Galatea, added in 1983, is where Dalí spent his final years.

Casa Museu Dalí

This magnificent seaside complex was Dalí's residence and sanctuary, where he lived with Gala from 1930 to 1982. The splendid whitewashed structure is a mishmash of cottages and sunny terraces, linked by narrow labyrinthine corridors and containing an assortment of offbeat furnishings.

The cottage was originally a mere fisherman's hut, but was steadily altered and enlarged by the Dalís. Every corner reveals a new and wondrous folly or objet d'art: a bejewelled taxidermied polar bear, stuffed swans (something of an obsession for Dalí) perched on bookshelves, and the echoing, womblike Oval Room. The artist's workshop, containing two unfinished original works, is especially interesting. Meanwhile, Dalí's bedroom still has a suspended mirror, positioned to ensure he was the first person to see the sunrise each morning. The dressing room, decorated by Gala, is covered in photos of the couple with high-profile acquaintances including Picasso, Coco Chanel and even Franco.

Castell de Púbol

If you're intrigued by Dalí, the Castell de Púbol is an essential piece of the puzzle. Between Girona and Palafrugell, this

Above Castell de Púbol; Right Teatre-Museu Dalí

14th-century castle was Dalí's gift to his wife and muse, Gala. The Castell de Púbol was her retreat from Dalí's whirlwind existence, and it offers teasing insights into the shared life of surrealism's most famous couple. It forms the southernmost point of the Dalí Triangle and is almost an antithesis to the flamboyance of the other two sites.

Gala married literary giant Éluard and took Dadaist artist Max Ernst as a lover, before moving on to Dalí. Although they married, Gala's dalliances didn't stop. In fact, the prospect of his charismatic wife playing away was thrilling to Dalí. Besotted with Gala, he was delighted by the idea of giving her a place to 'reign like an absolute sovereign'. In 1969, he bought the medieval castle, decorating it according to Gala's tastes. Ornamenting the Gothic-meets-Renaissance chateau with antiques and hand-painted ceilings was a labour of love. Velvet drapes and candelabra still decorate its walls, while a lip-shaped sofa and fountains with anglerfish statues add dashes of surreality. Gala would only allow Dalí permission to visit the Castell de Púbol if he submitted a hand-written request. The palace eventually became Gala's tomb. After her burial in its basement, Salvador used the castle as an artist's studio, hoping to channel his muse from the beyond.

To read about:
Architecture of the Imagination see page 164
Picasso's Art & War see page 194

Spanish Cinema

SPAIN-WIDE ART

Kiss goodbye to big-budget action block-busters and saccharine Hollywood rom-coms and enter the wonderfully offbeat world of Spanish cinema. Ever since iconoclastic filmmaker Luis Buñuel teamed up with surrealist artist Salvador Dalí in 1929 to make the bafflingly illogical silent short film Un chien andalou *(An Andalusian Dog), Spanish movies have sought to shock, surprise and bend genres.*

Right **Luis Buñuel**

Surrealistic Beginnings

Spain's early forays into the nascent art of film-making were ground-breaking and transgressive. It is a theme that continues to this day, spearheaded by directors who prefer to work more as independent auteurs than slaves to the big studio system.

Luis Buñuel, a leading member of Spain's surrealist movement in the 1920s, is generally considered to be the grandfather of Spanish film, the seed from which all else is descended. *Un chien andalou* is considered one of the most influential silent films of all time. Yet, after a dramatic opening salvo, Spain's flirtation with experimental film came to an abrupt halt with the advent of the civil war and the ascendency of Franco and censorship. Many artists, Buñuel included, emigrated, although the Aragonese director continued to make sporadic classics, including the French-produced *The Discreet Charm of the Bourgeoisie*, which won an Oscar for best foreign language film in 1972.

Back in Spain, boundary-pushing creativity practically dried up in the Franco era, although, by the 1970s, savvy directors had started to slip subtle protest past the censors. The most evocative and famous movie of the age was *El espíritu de la colmena* (The Spirit of the Beehive; 1973), the directorial debut of Victor Erice, a story about a young girl haunted by Frankenstein that clearly alluded to other 'monsters' in nationalist Spain.

Almodóvar & La Movida

It took the death of Franco in 1975 to spark an artistic reawakening in Spain. The renaissance, which was centred on Madrid and known as *la movida madrileña*, was epitomised by the irreverent film director Pedro Almodóvar from Castilla-La Mancha. Almodóvar's films were highly stylised pieces of art that mixed comedy, melodrama, homosexuality, kitsch, religion and strong, independent female characters. Like Buñuel before him, Almodóvar was not afraid to shock. He gained international recognition with *Mujeres al borde de un ataque de nervios* (Women on the Verge of a Nervous Breakdown; 1988) and went on to win Oscars for *Todo sobre mi madre* (All About My Mother) and *Hable con ella* (Talk to Her) in the 1990s and 2000s.

Going International

Several actors who have worked regularly with Almodóvar over the years have gone on to wider international success, most notably Penelope Cruz, who has appeared in seven of the director's films, and Antonio Banderas, who got his acting breakthrough in *Laberinto de pasiones* (Labyrinth of Passion) in 1982.

Another star, Javier Bardem, got his big break alongside an 18-year-old Cruz (whom he later married) in the flick *Jamón jamón*, a typically unconventional Spanish love story directed by Bigas Luna that culminated in a fight scene between two romantic rivals armed with legs of cured ham.

In the slipstream of Almodóvar's success other films quickly emerged. Some of the more memorable international hits proved to be equally marketable in the English-speaking world. Spanish-Chilean writer and director Alejandro Amenábar has flirted with a wide number of genres from sci-fi to horror. His critically acclaimed 1997 picture, *Abre los ojos* (Open Your Eyes), starring Penelope Cruz, was remade in English as *Vanilla Sky* four years later with Cruz reprising her role opposite Tom Cruise. *Mar adentro* (The Sea Inside), starring Javier Bardem, followed the true-life story of a quadriplegic Spanish man fighting for his right to die. *The Others* (2001), Amenábar's eerie horror movie starring Nicole Kidman, was the first solely English-speaking film to win a Spanish Goya award.

English-language Spanish-made films are by no means rare these days, with director Isabel Coixet having directed several. Her most recent film, *The Bookshop* (2017), starred British actors Bill Nighy and Emily Mortimer and was shot in Northern Ireland as well as Coixet's native Barcelona.

Pan's Labyrinth

Marking what is possibly the peak of Spanish cinema in recent years, *El laberinto del fauno* (Pan's Labyrinth) is a dark fantasy drama sometimes referred to as a fairy tale for adults. The film revisits the Franco era, mixing fantasy with post–civil war angst. Directed by Mexican Guillermo del Toro, it won three Oscars at the 2007 Academy Awards. While certainly the most lavish Spanish-made film in modern times, the movie also managed to maintain a refreshing level of independence, drawing heavily on its director's fertile imagination. Del Toro has subsequently gone on to even greater success, bagging Oscars for best film and best director with the American-made *The Shape of Water* in 2017.

To read about:
Master of Illusion: Salvador Dalí see page 170
Killing the Night see page 276

Game of Thrones on Location

Though set in the invented kingdom of Westeros, the hit fantasy television series has since 2010 showcased many scenic real-world locations. The show doubles as a whistle-stop introduction to a number of Spain's most stunning under-the-radar destinations.

To read about:

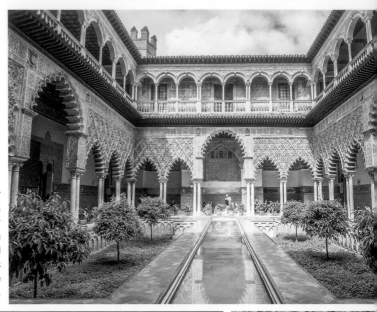

Right Seville's Real Alcázar
With 10th-century roots, Seville's fabled complex is still a palace for the Spanish royal family, and a spectacular blend of Christian and Mudéjar architecture. It starred as the palace and gardens of Dorne from season 5 onwards.

Right Itálica
The evocative Roman ruins of ancient Itálica, in modern-day Santiponce in Andalucía, include a magnificent 20,000-seat amphitheatre, one of the largest ever built. It stood in for the Dragonpit of King's Landing, where Daenerys and Jon met Cersei to negotiate an alliance against the Army of the Dead at the end of season 7. Now the Roman city is again hosting a Game of Thrones shoot, this time for the show's final season.

Right San Juan de Gaztelugatxe
On the road between the small towns of Bakio and Bermeo is one of the most photographed features of the Basque coast: the small island of San Juan de Gaztelugatxe. Attached to the mainland by a short causeway, this rocky isle is topped by a hermitage. It was used as the location for Daenerys Targaryen's ancestral home of Dragonstone in season 7.

Left Los Barruecos

In the Cáceres province of Extremadura is the Monumento Natural Los Barruecos, a stirring landscape of beautiful boulders piled high along the shores of pretty natural lakes and with important (and picturesque) breeding colonies for white storks. The cinematic beauty of the park caught the producers' eyes and the epic battle scenes of season 7 were filmed here.

Above Castillo de Zafra

Located in Castilla-La Mancha, this 12th-century castle was built on a sandstone outcrop in the province of Guadalajara. It was featured in season 6 as the Tower of Joy in the Red Mountains of Dorne.

Underwater Treasures: Museo Atlántico

CANARY ISLANDS ART

Europe's first underwater sculpture museum provides visitors with an otherworldly experience. In the depths of Playa Blanca off the coast of Lanzarote in the Canary Islands, this cultural marine gallery packs a powerful punch, with its warnings of environmental degradation in the form of sculpture.

Right *Crossing the Rubicon* by Jason de Caires Taylor at Museo Atlántico Lanzarote

At a depth of about 12m, Museo Atlántico acts as a breeding site for local marine species, and protects the marine environment by creating an artificial reef from the high-density, PH-neutral sculptures. Since the works were installed in 2016 there's been an increase in marine biomass, which is expected to grow each year.

The more than 300 large-scale installations and sculptures by British artist Jason de Caires Taylor, which can be explored by divers or seen from glass-bottomed boats, deliver a poignant message about our reliance on the ocean to survive and the effects of climate change. One piece, *Crossing the Rubicon*, is a huge installation consisting of 35 figures walking towards an underwater boundary. The final exhibit in Museo Atlántico is *The Human Gyre*, 200 life-size supine figures placed in a circle, providing a complex reef formation for marine life to inhabit.

To read about:

Picasso's Art & War see page 194
The Natural Art of Lanzarote see page 212

Pintxos Route in the Basque Country

BASQUE COUNTRY FOOD & DRINK

The Basque Country is widely considered one of the world's most exciting culinary destinations. Nearly 40 restaurants in the region have earned Michelin stars, with the highest concentration in San Sebastián. Gastronomic superstardom comes as second nature to the people of this region, where even the local tapas – known as pintxos – are like art on a plate.

There may be bigger and better-known culinary hot spots, but few cities are as food crazy as San Sebastián (known as Donostia in the Basque language). Set on an idyllic bay, this gracious belle époque resort is a food lover's dream date, offering everything from multi-Michelin-starred restaurants to magnificent *pintxos* and stunning seafood.

The city has long been a bastion of Basque culture, and its vibrant food scene reflects that. Culinary traditions, safeguarded by the city's unique gastronomic societies, are deeply entrenched even as they're being updated for the 21st century. The *nueva cocina vasca* (new Basque cuisine) movement emerged here in the late 1970s, and today the city's trailblazing chefs continue to innovate and push boundaries. As a result, San

Sebastián and its environs boast a large share of the world's top 20 restaurants and more Michelin stars per capita than almost anywhere else on earth. But eating well here is not all about multicourse tasting menus and haute cuisine. One of the city's quintessential experiences is bar crawling around the Parte Vieja (Old Quarter), filling up on *pintxos*. These magnificent one-plate wonders are a central feature of the city's culinary landscape and are enjoyed as much by socialising locals as visiting tourists.

Fuelling San Sebastián's insatiable appetite for fine food is a ready supply of fresh ingredients. From the sea come *antxoas* (anchovies), *merluza* (hake) and *bacalao* (salted cod), a mainstay since it was introduced by Basque fishing folk in the 15th century. Inland, verdant hills

provide lush grazing ground for livestock – *txuleta* steak is a prized Basque speciality – and a rich assortment of seasonal fruit and veg.

Kafe Botanika

Before embarking on your culinary adventures, treat yourself to breakfast at this laid-back San Sebastián cafe. Housed in a residential block by the river, it's a popular spot with a leafy courtyard and a sunny, art-filled interior. The cafe specialises in vegetarian food and has many local fans. If you don't make it for breakfast, come late afternoon, when everyone from parents with toddlers to laptop-wielding students and gossiping shoppers stops by for a coffee or glass of something stronger.

Mercado de la Bretxa

After breakfast follow the river down to the Parte Vieja and, on its eastern side, the Mercado de la Bretxa. The market, which is centred on a small, neoclassical shopping mall, is serious foodie territory and many local chefs come to stock up on their daily provisions. Outside, farmers' stalls are laden with brightly coloured regional produce: tomatoes from neighbouring Getaria, black Tolosa beans, *guindilla* peppers from Ibarra, *idiazábal* cheese. Inside, in the basement of the main building, local fishmongers put on an impressive display with trays full of monkfish, Aguinaga elvers (young eels), hake and, of course, the omnipresent *bacalao*. Also in the basement you'll find richly stocked butchers' stalls adorned with hanging *jamón* (ham) and strings of Basque *chistorras* (cured sausages).

Mimo San Sebastián

For a memorable introduction to the local cuisine, sign up for a class at Mimo San Sebastián's gleaming cooking school. One of the most popular courses, and one of several to include a guided market visit, is the Pintxo Masterclass. Led by expert Basque chefs, this hands-on session covers the tricks and techniques behind some of the city's trademark *pintxos*, including the legendary 'Gilda'. This spicy combination of anchovies, *manzanilla* olives and *guindilla* peppers was created in 1946 at the Bar Casa Vallés and named after the Rita Hayworth film, which was a big hit at the time and one of the few 'hot' movies to have survived Franco's censorship. The cooking school is a short walk south of Bretxa market.

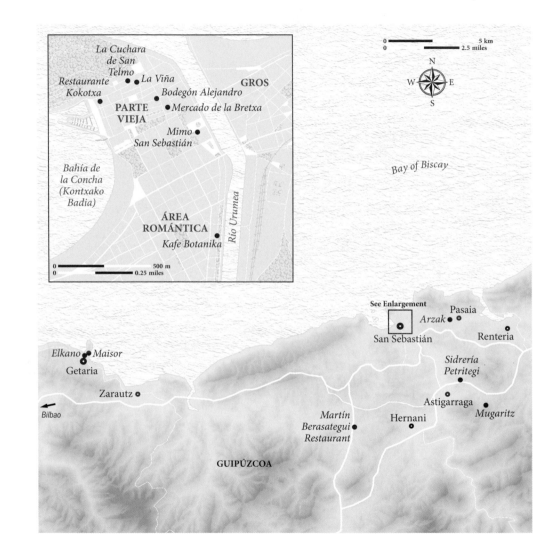

Meals of a Lifetime

Serious foodies plan entire trips around an evening at one of the Basque Country's three-Michelin-star venues. But the one-star restaurants are usually more affordable and accessible. Reservations are essential!

Arzak This San Sebastián restaurant is the home kitchen of Spain's most revered father-daughter team. With three shining stars, acclaimed chef Juan Mari Arzak is king when it comes *to nueva cocina vasca*.

Martín Berasategui Restaurant This superlative triple-starred restaurant outside San Sebastián is led by chef Martín Berasategui, who approaches cuisine as a science, creating tastes you never knew existed.

Mugaritz In the hills south of San Sebastián is this unforgettable dining experience: a 24-course tasting menu with edible cutlery. With two stars, it's slightly more accessible (for the time being).

Mina This one-star riverside institution in Bilbao is known for its culinary creativity. The menu swings toward the avant-garde: a popular dessert is frozen 'seawater' with seaweed and lemon sorbet.

Restaurante Kokotxa The chefs of this one-star venue shop daily at San Sebastián's colourful market, creating special *menús de mercado* (market menus) – fresh, unique and always changing.

La Cuchara de San Telmo

For a rousing finale to your day, explore the Parte Vieja with a *pintxos* bar crawl. One of the joys of eating in San Sebastián is that you don't have to dine at a Michelin-starred restaurant to sample superb contemporary cuisine. If you know where to go, you can tuck into innovative high-end food for no more than the price of a drink. Take this place: a small, un-fussy bar that serves superb cooked-to-order *pintxos*. Dishes such as *carrillera de ternera al vino tinto* (calf's cheeks braised in red wine) and *foie salteado con compota de manzana* (foie gras with apple compote) are mini-masterpieces of modern Basque cooking with superb ingredients and sumptuous flavours.

La Viña

Ask a local and they'll tell you that the art to a successful bar crawl is to have one, maximum two, *pintxos* at any one place. Most bars have their own speciality and that's the one to go for. Just down the road from La Cuchara, La Viña is a traditional wood-clad bar that's been in the same family since it opened in 1959. It serves excellent seafood *pintxos* but its main claim to fame is its celebrated *tarta de queso* (cheesecake). Every morning batches of this wobbly, caramel-coloured delicacy are cooked and left to cool in baking tins strewn across the bar. The recipe is a closely guarded secret but whatever they make them with, the result-ing cakes are sublime: light, creamy and sweet without ever being too cloying. The *tarta* will round off your day nicely but, quite frankly, it's pretty fabulous any time.

Bodegón Alejandro

The next day, head back to the Parte Vieja for a sit-down lunch affair at this casu-al, much-lauded restaurant. Bodegón Alejandro is part of local food history: it was here that the triple-Michelin-starred chef Martín Berasategui got his first taste of kitchen life, working alongside his mum and aunt in what was then his parents' restaurant. Nowadays it's one of several eateries managed by Andoni Luis Aduriz, the superstar chef-patron of Mugaritz. And while the menu here is more down to earth, chef Inaxio Valverde cooks a very popular line in Basque seafood.

Sidrería Petritegi

The Basque Country has long been a centre of cider production (*txotx* in Basque). Records refer to it as far back as the 11th century, and it's said that in the 17th and 18th centuries Basque seafarers would take more cider than water on their ships in the hope that the vitamins it contained would stave off scurvy. To test its medicinal properties for yourself, head to Sidrería Petritegi, a traditional cider house in the hills 5km southeast of San Sebastián. One of the few cider houses open year-round – most fling their doors wide from January to April when the annual batch of cider is cracked open – it offers guided tours and tastings, as well as a classic cider-house menu. But the star of the show is the strong, still cider, which bartenders skilfully squirt from huge bar-rels directly into your tankard. Be warned, though, it can get messy, and as the cider flows, be prepared for the fact that your night might end in a drenching.

Maisor

Some 25km west of San Sebastián, Getar-ia is a charming fishing village renowned for its seafood restaurants and *txakoli* wine. This sparkling white is produced in the nearby hills and, with its low alcohol content and crisp dry flavour, makes an ideal accompaniment for *pintxos*. But it's the sea that's the historical lifeblood of Getaria, and its fishing fleet continues to ply the cold Cantabrian waters trawling for turbot, mackerel, sea bream and sardines. A local speciality is anchovies, salt-cured and preserved by hand at Maisor, a family-run canning outfit down at the harbour. Maisor is open for guided visits (during shop opening times but best on weekday mornings) and runs hands-on workshops (reservations required) where you can learn all about the traditional techniques they use to salt, bone and pack the fish.

Elkano

Round off your visit to Getaria with a meal at Elkano, a much-revered local institution. This superb seafood restaurant has been thrilling diners since 1964 and under its second-generation owner, Aitor Arregui, it earned its first Michelin star. Unlike many of the area's starred eateries, it's kept things traditional and still specialises in seasonal fish prepared with disarming simplicity. Its signature dish, *rodaballo* (turbot), is cooked on an open-air charcoal grill, served whole. Another Basque clas-sic to try is *kokotxas pil pil,* hake throats served in an emulsion of their own gelatin, with olive oil, parsley and garlic.

To read about:

Tortilla: Spanish Omelette see page 66
Kalimotxo see page 186

Kalimotxo: An Iconic Summer Cocktail

Guaranteed to have wine purists up in arms, this cheeky beverage is a mix of red wine and cola. It's refreshing, cheap and championed by many – especially Spanish teenagers.

Some may have doubts about this drink, especially given its reputation as the drink of choice for the younger set; they are known for buying the harshest of wines and swishing it together with Coca-Cola in a plastic bag at *botellones* (impromptu street gatherings). However, on a sizzling summer night, surrounded by a boisterous crowd at a Spanish festival, it all starts to make sense. Like the festival itself, the drink is cheerful and unfussy – and incredibly popular. It comes in a plastic glass loaded with ice. For a few euros it's immediately satisfying: the sugar and caffeine pep you up, but are balanced by the mellowing effect of the wine. How else are you expected to last well into the next morning?

Originally known as a *Rioja Libre* or *Cuba Libre del pobre* (poor man's Cuba Libre) in 1970s Spain, its current name was later coined at a Basque festival. According to legend, its creators realised they were serving bad wine and decided to disguise the taste by mixing it with Coke; the drink became an unlikely hit. Named after their two friends, Kalimero and Motxo, it's popular throughout Spain and is an icon of Basque culture.

To read about:
On the Grapevine: La Rioja see page 50
The Hour of Vermouth see page 272

Kalimotxo

Ingredients
→ 1L red wine (preferably strong and dry, of the cheaper variety)
→ 1L cola
→ ice
→ slice of lemon (optional)

Method
Mix equal parts of the red wine and cola. Serve with ice. If you want to spice up this simple drink you could add a slice of lemon, but *kalimotxo* purists – if they even exist – may disagree.

Bucking Tradition: The Bullfighting Debate

There is no more controversial activity in Spain than bullfighting. Already effectively banned in three of the country's autonomous communities (Catalonia and the Balearic and Canary Islands), this deeply rooted traditional activity has faced mounting opposition in recent years. But the ritual of bullfighting remains strong in some parts of Spain, notably Andalucía, Madrid, Castilla y León and Castilla-La Mancha.

Right **The Osborne Bull**

Steeped in tradition, bullfighting has changed little in essentials since its inception, and its supporters emphasise historical legacy and its high-profile place in Spanish culture. Some claim that *corridas* (bullfights) are less cruel than slaughterhouses. For its opponents, however, bullfighting is an intolerably cruel, violent spectacle that sees many thousands of bulls slowly and painfully killed in public every year, and they consider it a blight on Spain's conscience in these supposedly more enlightened times.

An opinion poll in December 2015 found that only 19% of Spaniards aged between 16 and 65 supported bullfighting, while 58% opposed it. Among 16- to 24-year-olds, the level of support was just 7%. These days, the number of *corridas* in Spanish bullrings is falling dramatically, with a reported decline from 3651 bullfights in 2007 to 1598 in 2016, according to government figures.

A ban on bullfighting became law in Catalonia in 2012, and a number of mainly left-wing local councils in various other regions have stopped bullfighting in their areas. Large anti-bullfighting demonstrations happen regularly in Madrid, but there have also been demonstrations supporting bullfighting. The pro-bullfighting lobby remains strong, and attributes the decline in number of *corridas* partly to economic recession.

That there is a debate at all about the morality of bullfighting owes much to Spain's growing integration with the rest of Europe since its return to democracy in the late 1970s. Much of the anti-bullfighting impetus has come from groups beyond Spanish shores, but home-grown pro-animal-rights organisations are ever more active.

The Osborne Bull

Bulls have become part of Spanish culture in more than just the *corridas*. A certain legendary black-bull logo is found on souvenirs and flags, and visitors can hardly miss the sight of it on life-sized billboards all over the country. But this icon's origin is less well known than its appearance.

Englishman Thomas Osborne Mann befriended local winegrowers in El Puerto de Santa María in 1772, and set up what is today one of Spain's oldest family sherry firms, Bodegas Osborne.

In the 1950s Osborne started an advertising campaign that saw the creation of its black-bull logo and the dotting of the Spanish landscape with the famous billboards. In the 1980s, roadside advertising was banned throughout the country, but popular support gained a pardon for the Toro de Osborne in the 1990s, on the condition that the brand name be removed. The ruling states that the Osborne Bull 'has gone beyond its initial advertising purpose and has become part of the landscape'. And so the bull's silhouette marks journeys throughout Spain to this day.

To read about:

Gloriously Gay Sitges

CATALONIA PEOPLE & CULTURE

It's no surprise that Sitges is such an LGBT favourite. This elegant beach resort in Catalonia has long had a liberal air, being a key location for the Modernisme movement and the home of artists and creatives. That forward-thinking vibe along with its gorgeous beaches, good-looking architecture, buzzing nightlife, upmarket restaurants and chic boutiques mean it's Spain's most famous gay holiday destination and is set to stay that way.

Right **Carnaval**

Gloriously Gay Nightlife

Sitges' gay scene is geographically small, but what it lacks in size it makes up for with energy and atmosphere in spades. Start your night with a drink at gay stalwart Parrots on Plaça de la Indústria: punters sit at outward-facing tables, checking out the latest talent in town (it's all part of the fun). After you've downed your G&T, head up Carrer de Joan Tarrida, which is home to most of the town's LGBT venues and by midnight is always thronged with drinkers. If you're after something civilised, La Villa is a classy little bar with a lovely verdant courtyard garden out back.

For late-night bars you can dance in, pop round the corner to Carrer de Bonaire and try Privilege, artfully strewn with stages and poles where you can strike a pose; or over the street, even-more-lively Queenz is mobbed every night in summer. Lovely bar staff serve drinks that pack a punch and the DJ spins nonstop pop hits. To carry on your night until morning, the best club option is Organic, which in summer plays host to twice-weekly foam parties.

Beach Bliss

Bassa Rodona, immediately west of the town centre, is Sitges' famous unofficial gay beach, though LGBT sunbathers are now spread out pretty evenly across the town's stretches of sand. A kilometre northeast of the centre lies sheltered Balmins, favoured by nudists; a mixed crowd comes here, but it's definitely a gay favourite.

A popular stop on a Sitges itinerary is a day at L'Home Mort, a gay clothing-optional beach in a sheltered cove about an hour's walk west of central Sitges. The journey there is all part of the fun, with lovely views back over town from the headland east of the beach.

Fabulous Festivals

Carnaval in Sitges is a sparkly, week-long, booze-soaked riot every February or March, complete with masked balls and capped by lavish parades held on the Sunday and Tuesday, featuring immaculately dressed drag queens, huge sound systems and a wild all-night party with bars staying open until dawn.

Sitges Pride is also a big event on the town's gay calendar, taking place over 10 hard-partying days in early June. A huge Sunday afternoon parade along the seafront is the centrepiece, but the festivities also see open-air concerts and parties at the beachside Pride Village every night, as well as daytime shenanigans in the form of boat and pool parties.

The town's other notable gay party is Bears Week every September, which draws hairy dudes and their admirers from far and wide.

To read about:

La Tomatina see page 40
Killing the Night see page 276

Cycling the Railways of Andalucía

Spain's greatest environmental idea in the last 20 years might just be its vías verdes (greenways): decommissioned railway lines that have been transformed into designated paths for cyclists, walkers and other nonmotorised transport, including wheelchairs. Spain has 7500km of abandoned railway track, and since 1993, 2100km of it has been converted into vías verdes.

Aside from their natural attractions (bird reserves, olive groves), the *vías* guard uncommon chapters of human history. The Vía Verde del Aceite (Jaén province) once carried olive oil to the coast for export; the Vía Verde de Riotinto (Huelva province) ferried miners to the famous opencast Rio Tinto mines. Many of the original engineering features have been preserved, including bridges, viaducts, tunnels and stations, some of which have been converted into cafes or rural hotels that hire out bikes.

Vía Verde de la Sierra

Andalucía's finest greenway is often considered to be the Vía Verde de la Sierra (Cádiz). The 36km greenway between Olvera and Puerto Serrano (to the west) boasts the wild, rugged scenery of Spain's south. This route is notable for four spectacular viaducts, 30 tunnels (some with sensor-activated lighting) and three old stations transformed into hotel-restaurants. The train line itself was never actually completed: it was constructed in the late 1920s as part of the abortive Jerez–Almargen railway, but the Spanish Civil War put a stop to construction works. The line was restored in the early 2000s.

A highlight of the *vía* is the Peñón de Zaframagón, a distinctive crag that's a prime breeding ground for griffon vultures. The Centro de Interpretación y Observatorio Ornitológico, in the former Zaframagón station building 16km west of Olvera, allows close-up observations of the birds by means of a high-definition camera placed up on the crag.

Vía Verde del Aceite

Some 120km of disused railway, including three tunnels, 13 viaducts and 12 old stations, run across the olive-strewn countryside of southern Jaén and Córdoba provinces (and close to Córdoba's Sierras Subbéticas mountains) on this well-surfaced cycling and walking track. With gentle gradients and refreshment stops en route, it makes for an enjoyable extended ride.

Vía Verde de la Sierra Norte

This 18km cycling (and walking) route is one of the most popular of Andalucía's 23 *vías verdes*. Running along a disused mining railway, it leads north through the Huéznar valley below Cazalla to the village of San Nicolás del Puerto and on south to the old Cerro del Hierro mines.

To read about:
A Rock Climber's Paradise see page 208
Cycle the City see page 258

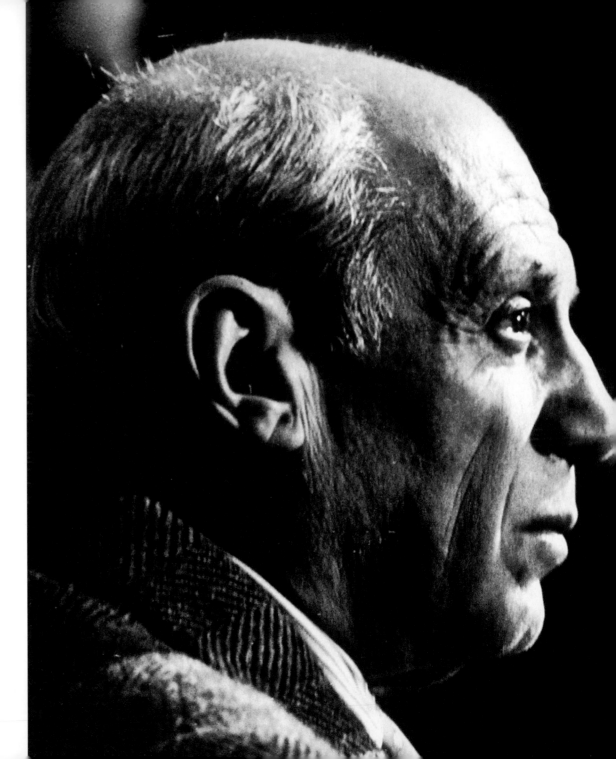

Picasso's Art & War

In the early years of the 20th century, the genius of the mischievous malagueño *(Málaga native) Pablo Ruiz Picasso (1881–1973) came like a thunderclap. Picasso was formed in an atmosphere laden with the avant-garde freedom of Modernisme. He must have been one of the most restless artists of all time. His work underwent repeated revolutions as he passed from one creative phase to another. From his gloomy Blue Period through the brighter Pink Period and on to cubism, Picasso was nothing if not surprising.*

Picasso in Málaga

Perhaps understandably for a boy baptised with a dozen (mostly saints' and relatives') names, Picasso became famous for signing his paintings with just one. Born in Málaga to Don José Ruíz y Blasco (also an artist) and María Picasso y López, the young Pablo lived in Málaga until he was 10. In 1891 he moved with his family to A Coruña in Galicia. Since he never returned permanently to Málaga, Picasso's connection with Andalucía was long underemphasised; you'll find better exhibitions of his art in Barcelona and Paris. But with Málaga undergoing a cultural awakening in recent decades, the city has taken steps to reclaim him.

Museo Picasso Málaga

The Picasso Foundation was established in 1988 in Picasso's Casa Natal (birth house) in Plaza de la Merced, and, in 2003, after 50 years of on-off planning, the excellent Museo Picasso Málaga was opened in a 16th-century palace. This unmissable museum provides a solid overview of the great master and his work. The 200-plus works in the collection were donated and loaned to the museum by Christine Ruiz-Picasso (wife of Paul, Picasso's eldest son) and Bernard Ruiz-Picasso (Picasso's grandson) and catalogue the artist's sparkling career with a few notable gaps (the Blue and Pink Periods are largely missing). Nonetheless, numerous gems adorn the gallery's lily-white walls. Highlights include a painting of Picasso's sister Lola undertaken when the artist was only 13; sculptures made from clay, plaster and sheet metal; numerous sketches; a quick journey through cubism; and some interesting late works when Picasso developed an obsession with musketeers.

Picasso in Barcelona

In 1895 a teenage Picasso moved to Barcelona. It was here that he spent his time ceaselessly drawing and painting, and ultimately established his artistic reputation. Picasso lived and worked in the Barri Gòtic and El Raval (where he was introduced to the seamier side of life in the Barri Xinès). Some of his portraits and cityscapes were created in and inspired by what he saw in Barcelona. A number of pieces from this period hang in the Museu Picasso.

Museu Picasso

Barcelona's Museu Picasso is strongest on Picasso's earliest years, up until 1904, which is apt considering that the artist spent his formative creative years here. Allegedly it was Picasso himself who proposed the museum's creation in 1960, to his friend and personal secretary Jaume Sabartés, a Barcelona native. Three years later, the 'Sabartés Collection' was opened, since a museum bearing Picasso's name would have been met with censorship – Picasso's opposition to the Franco regime was well known. The Museu Picasso we see today opened in 1983. From Sabartés' personal collection of Picasso's art and a handful of works hanging at the Barcelona Museum of Art, the collection gradually expanded with donations from Salvador Dalí and Sebastià Junyer Vidal, among others, though the largest part of the present collection came from Picasso himself. His widow, Jacqueline Roque, also donated 41 ceramic pieces and the *Woman with Bonnet* painting after Picasso's death.

While the collection in the Museu Picasso concentrates on the artist's formative years – sometimes disappointing for those hoping for a feast of his better-known later works (they had better head for Paris) – there is enough material from subsequent periods to give you a thorough impression of the man's versatility and genius. Above all, you come away feeling that Picasso was the true original, always one step ahead of himself (let alone anyone else), in his search for new forms of expression.

Picasso in Madrid

Although Picasso spent much of his working life in Paris, he arrived in Madrid from Barcelona in 1897 at the behest of his father for a year's study at the Escuela de Bellas Artes de San Fernando. Never one to allow himself to be confined within formal structures, the precocious Picasso instead took himself to the Museo del Prado to learn from the masters, and to the streets to depict life as he saw it. Picasso went on to become the master of cubism, which was inspired by his fascination with primitivism, primarily African masks and early Iberian sculpture. This highly complex form reached its high point in *Guernica* (1937).

Centro de Arte Reina Sofía & Guernica

Home to Picasso's *Guernica,* arguably Spain's most famous artwork, the Centro de Arte Reina Sofía is Madrid's premier collection of contemporary art. In addition to plenty of paintings by Picasso, other major drawcards are works by Salvador Dalí and Joan Miró.

Claimed by some to be the most important artwork of the 20th century, *Guernica* measures 3.5m by 7.8m and

Above **Pablo Picasso statue by Francisco López Hernández; Right Museu Picasso**, Barcelona

is astounding in the detail of its various constituent elements. It has always been a controversial work and was initially derided by many as being more propaganda than art. After the Spanish Civil War broke out in 1936, Picasso had been commissioned by the Republican government in Madrid to do a painting for the Paris Exposition Universelle in 1937. As news filtered out about the bombing of Gernika (as it is spelled in the Basque language), Picasso committed his anger to canvas. To understand the painting's earthshattering impact at the time, it must be remembered that the attack on Gernika represented the first use of airborne military hardware to devastating effect. Thus it was that this signature work of cubism's disfiguration of the human form would become an eloquent symbol of a world's outrage at the horrors wrought upon the innocent by modern warfare.

Guernica subsequently migrated to the USA and only returned to Spain in 1981, in keeping with Picasso's wish that the painting return to Spanish shores once democracy had been restored. Basques believe that its true home is in the Basque Country and calls to have it moved there continue unabated. Such a move is, however, unlikely to happen any time soon, with the Reina Sofía arguing that the painting is too fragile to be moved again.

To read about:

Basque Culture see page 64
Madrid Through the Eyes of an Artist see page 264

Adventure

Exploring Wild Spain

Few countries in Europe can match Spain's diversity of landscapes. For those who prefer their journey with a dash of adrenalin, Spain is a wonderful adventure playground.

The country is famous for superb walking trails that criss-cross mountains and hills, from the Pyrenees and Picos de Europa to the sultry Cabo de Gata coastal trail in Andalucía. To walk in mountain villages, the classic spot is Las Alpujarras, near the Sierra Nevada in Andalucía, while the Pyrenean foothills in Navarra and Aragón offer superb village-to-village hiking. Hiking is possible year-round, but summer is the only time to hike the high mountains.

Hiking may get all the headlines, but there's so much more. Surfing (from the Basque Country to the Costa de la Luz), kitesurfing (Tarifa), skiing, horse riding, snorkelling and rock climbing – it's all possible here.

Nearly 10% of the country is protected in some way but most of these stirring wilderness areas remain accessible to those with a spirit of adventure. Spain has nine national parks on the mainland and one on the Balearic Islands, and the country ranks among Europe's premier wildlife-watching destinations. There are bears in Cantabria and elsewhere, wolves roam the hill country of western Castilla y León, while down south, the resurgence of the endangered Iberian lynx is one of the great success stories in the annals of modern conservation. Birdlife is another reason why lovers of wildlife can't get enough of Spain.

But it's not all about leg-power and wildlife: volcanic landscapes, epic train journeys, thrilling festivals and foodie excursions into the Catalan backcountry are also ways to take a walk on Spain's wild side.

Hiking the Powerful Pyrenees

The Pyrenees, separating Spain from France, are Spain's premier walking destination. The range is utterly beautiful: prim and chocolate-box pretty on the lower slopes, wild and bleak at higher elevations, and relatively unspoilt compared to some European mountain ranges. It's tough but rewarding terrain, a world of great rock walls and glacial cirques, accompanied by elusive but soulful Pyrenean wildlife.

The Pyrenees aren't Europe's highest mountains, but they are certainly among its most formidable. The craggy behemoths stretch from the Bay of Biscay to the Mediterranean like a giant wall, with barely a low-level pass to break them. Spectacular for many reasons, not least the abundance of powerful waterfalls, they act like a siren's call for hikers.

Anyone who hikes in the Spanish Pyrenees will get on to first-name terms with Gran Recorrido 11 (GR11), the long-distance footpath that runs along the range's entire Spanish flank from Hondarribia on the Bay of Biscay to Cap de Creus on the Costa Brava. Approximately 820km long and with a cumulative elevation gain equivalent to five Mt Everests, it takes around 45 days even without rest days. Many people elect to walk it in a series of shorter hops. Well-frequented sections run along Aragón's Valle de Ordesa and past Catalonia's Estany de Sant Maurici.

June to October are generally the best months for hiking. There may be snow on passes and high valleys until mid-June or from October, and the weather is never predictable, so walkers should always be prepared for extreme conditions. However, since this is Europe (rather than Alaska), you're never too far from a mountain village with basic shops, bars and accommodation. Up in the mountains are a variety of refugios (refugis in Catalan) – some staffed and serving meals, others providing shelter only.

Day Hikes

There are countless superb hikes in Parque Nacional de Ordesa y Monte Perdido. Wonderful full-day outings include the high-level Faja de Pelay path (to a waterfall) and the Balcón de Pineta route to a superb lookout point. This is where the Spanish Pyrenees really take your breath away. The wonderful scenery of plunging canyons, towering cliffs, thick forests, rivers, waterfalls, snow peaks, mountain lakes and high-level glaciers makes this arguably the place to head for if you can manage only one destination in the Spanish Pyrenees.

Aigüestortes i Estany de Sant Maurici, Catalonia's only national park, extends 20km east to west, and just 9km north to south, but the rugged mountain terrain within this small area sparkles with more than 200 lakes and countless streams and waterfalls, combined with pine and fir forests, and open bush decked with wildflowers or autumn leaves. Fit walkers can cross the Aigüestortes park in one day along the Sant Maurici–Boí traverse, a 22km sequence of lakes, waterfalls, verdant valleys, rocky peaks and inspiring vistas.

To read about:

Right Parque Nacional de Ordesa y Monte Perdido

El Caminito del Rey: The Path of the King

The most thrilling hike in southern Spain is the vertigo-inducing El Caminito del Rey (The Path of the King). The walk-way, which follows El Chorro gorge near Málaga, reopened in 2015 after being closed for over a decade due to fatalities along the route. The path has been com-prehensively upgraded and is no longer dangerous, but it still offers breathtaking views over the gorge that requires a head for heights.

To read about:

Call of the Wild

SPAIN-WIDE WILDLIFE

The howl of the wolf calls to mind snow-shrouded Arctic forests – less often sunlit plazas and pitchers of sangría. However, the north of Spain has always been a land apart from the rest of the country, and is home to the largest wolf population west of Russia. Indeed, from brown bears to mountain goats, endangered lynxes to birds, the country teems with wildlife. For a walk on the wild side, Spain is one of Europe's best destinations.

Right **Iberian wolves**

Most of the excitement surrounds the three flagship species – the Iberian wolf in the far north, the Iberian lynx in Andalucía, and the brown bear in the mountains of the Cordillera Cantábrica. But beyond these three await as many species as you can aim a camera at. They include ibex (stocky mountain goats with distinctive long horns), wild boar, deer, mongooses, genets (catlike creatures with white-and-black coats) and chamois (small antelope that live in the Pyrenees and Cordillera Cantábrica). Gibraltar's 'apes' – actually Barbary macaques – are the only wild monkeys in Europe. Twenty-seven marine mammal species live off Spain's shores, and dolphin- and whale-spotting boat trips are a popular attraction at Gibraltar and nearby Tarifa. Birdwatchers rave about the twitching possibilities in Spain, with flocks of migrating birds crossing Andalucía.

Iberian Wolf

Spain is home to Western Europe's largest contingent of wolves – an estimated 2000 to 2500 survive here. Spain's *lobo ibérico* (Iberian wolves) are largely restricted to the country's northwest. Though officially protected, wolves are still considered an enemy by many people and the hunting of wolves is still permitted in some areas.

The largest and most easily accessible wild wolf population is in the Sierra de Culebra, close to Zamora. Travellers keen to catch a glimpse of this captivating predator can join excursions with operators such as Zamora Natural or Wild Wolf Experience (though sightings can never be guaranteed). An interpretation centre devoted to the region and its wolves, the Centro de Lobo Ibérico de Castillo y León, is found in the small village of Robledo, around 8km southwest of Puebla de Sanabria.

Brown Bear

The wild mountain area of southwest Asturias and northwestern Castilla y León is the main stronghold of Spain's biggest animal, the *oso pardo* (brown bear). Bear numbers in the Cordillera Cantábrica have climbed to more than 250, from as low as 70 in the mid-1990s.

This charismatic beast can reach 300kg and live 25 to 30 years, and has traditionally been disliked by farmers, but public support has played a big part in its recent recovery. Experts warn that the bear population is not yet completely out of the woods – illegal snares and poisoned bait set for wild boar and wolves continue to pose serious threats, as do forest fires, new roads and ski stations, which reduce the bears' habitat and mobility.

The best place for travellers to see brown bears in the wild is the Parque Natural de Somiedo in southwestern Asturias, while there is also a very small chance of catching a glimpse of one in the Picos de Europa. You can see bears in semi-liberty at the Cercado Osero on the Senda del Oso (Path of the Bear), a popular cycling and walking track southwest of Oviedo. The Fundación Oso Pardo is Spain's major resource and advocate for brown bears and its Centro de Interpretación 'Somiedo y El Oso', in Pola de Somiedo, is a good place to brush up on bear facts and get closer to one than in the wild.

Iberian Lynx

The beautiful and elusive *lince ibérico* (Iberian lynx), Andalucía's most celebrated mammal, is one of the most endangered wild cat species on earth. It once inhabited large areas of the peninsula, but numbers fell below 100 at the beginning of the 21st century. The Iberian lynx has battled for survival against disastrous slumps in its main prey, the rabbit, since the 1950s, but also against hunters, developers, habitat loss and even tourism. Road traffic is a major threat.

But there's good news: Andalucía's lynx numbers are up. Most of the credit goes to an increasingly successful program of in-captivity breeding and release into the wild, along with the topping up of local rabbit populations. In June 2015 the Iberian lynx was taken off the IUCN (International Union for Conservation of Nature) 'critically endangered' list. In 2017 there were estimated to be some 500 Iberian lynxes in the wild; for now, at least, the future looks brighter for the lynx.

Almost all of Spain's wild lynxes prowl around Andalucía, split between the Parque Nacional de Doñana and the Sierra Morena. Unfortunately travellers would have to be exceptionally lucky to see one in the wild. Doñana's visitor centre, El Acebuche, streams a live video of lynxes in its nearby breeding centre, which makes for pretty exciting viewing even when they're just stretching, yawning and grooming themselves – but you can't visit them in person.

Birdlife

With around 500 species, Spain has easily the biggest and most varied bird population in Europe. Around 25 species of birds of prey, including the *águila real* (golden eagle), *buitre leonado* (griffon vulture) and *alimoche* (Egyptian vulture), breed here.

Spain's extensive wetlands make it a haven for water birds. The most important of the wetlands is the Parque Nacional de Doñana and surrounding areas in the Guadalquivir delta in Andalucía. Laguna de Fuente de Piedra, near Antequera, sees as many as 20,000 greater flamingo (*flamenco*) pairs rearing chicks in spring and summer.

The large, ungainly *cigüeña blanca* (white stork), actually black and white, nests from spring to summer on electricity pylons and in trees and towers across western Andalucía. Much rarer and less sociable is the *cigüeña negra* (black stork), which prefers cliff ledges. Both birds are mainly migrant visitors, crossing the Strait of Gibraltar from Africa to breed in Spain, although a few of them stay year-round.

To read about:

Spanish Sands see page 78
Cantabria's Prehistoric Cave Art see page 156

A Rock Climber's Paradise

Thanks to its mountainous topography and excellent weather, Spain has become recognised as Europe's best sport-climbing destination, particularly during winter. Stretching from the limestone gorge of El Chorro in Andalucía to the peaks of the Picos de Europa in Asturias, there is something for everyone. But perhaps the pick of the bunch is Catalonia, in particular, the area to the north of Lleida, which has the highest concentration of peaks in the region. Here you will find a roll call of the world's best crags: Oliana, Terradets, Riglos, Rodellar, to mention a few.

Right **Margalef**, Catalonia

Andalucía

Renowned El Chorro, a sheer limestone gorge above the Río Guadalhorce, contains hundreds of climbing routes, from easy to ultra-difficult. Many start in the vicinity of Caminito del Rey, a notoriously narrow path that clings to the rock face. Other crags are El Torcal de Antequera (Málaga) and Los Cahorros gorge (Sierra Nevada).

Vie ferrate – routes equipped with ladders, cables, bridges and ziplines – are increasingly popular in Andalucía. There are good beginner routes in Ronda and more advanced routes in El Torcal, El Chorro and Comares.

Mallorca

Mallorca's sublime limestone walls have climbers' hearts pounding. The island is among Europe's foremost destinations for sport climbers. Climbing here concentrates on three areas: the southwest for multi-pitch climbing, the northwest for magnificent crags and the east for superb deep water soloing (DWS).

A holy grail for climbers, Sa Gubia is a huge fist of rock combed with multi-pitch routes. Other hot spots include the ragged limestone crags of the Formentor peninsula and the coves of Porto Cristo and Cala Barques.

Riglos

Little Riglos, northwest of Huesca in Catalonia, sits at the foot of Los Mallos de Riglos, a set of awe-inspiring rock towers that dwarf the village. Los Mallos are a popular challenge for serious rock climbers – and popular too with the huge griffon vultures that nest here. Near the village is a plaque with a sobering list of climbers who perished climbing here.

Canyoning in Alquézar

For exhilarating descents into steep-walled canyons by any means possible (but in the care of professional guides), try Alquézar in Aragón, one of Europe's prime locations for this popular sport. Alquézar's activities operators can also arrange rock climbing and rafting in the area of the Sierra de Guara.

Canyoning is also possible in Cangas de Onís in the Picos de Europa, in the Sierra de Grazalema in Cádiz province, and the Pallars Sobirá area in the Catalan Pyrenees.

To read about:

The Mountains of Picos de Europa see page 98
El Caminito del Rey see page 202

Egg-splosive Flour War

Spain has its fair share of crazy festivals, but Els Enfarinats, held annually on 28 December, takes the cake for the messiest event. The residents of Ibi in Alicante (the Valencia region) declare a flour war between two opposing groups, with one group going around fining residents for made-up misdemeanours, while the opposing group unleashes flour bombs, eggs and firecrackers in a bid to restore order. At the end of the day, scenes of carnage and flour-covered streets are cleaned up, peace is reinstated and the fines are donated to charity. While the modern version has been running in its current form since 1981, no one knows the origins of the original fight, a 200-year-old tradition.

To read about:

The Natural Art of Lanzarote

A stark volcanic landscape dotted with whitewashed houses, a smattering of sculptures and unique architectural projects; the island of Lanzarote can appear to be one giant work of art. Both violent nature and the late artist César Manrique have left an inescapable impression on this wild land, one that continues to set it apart as a fascinating location.

Right **La Geria**

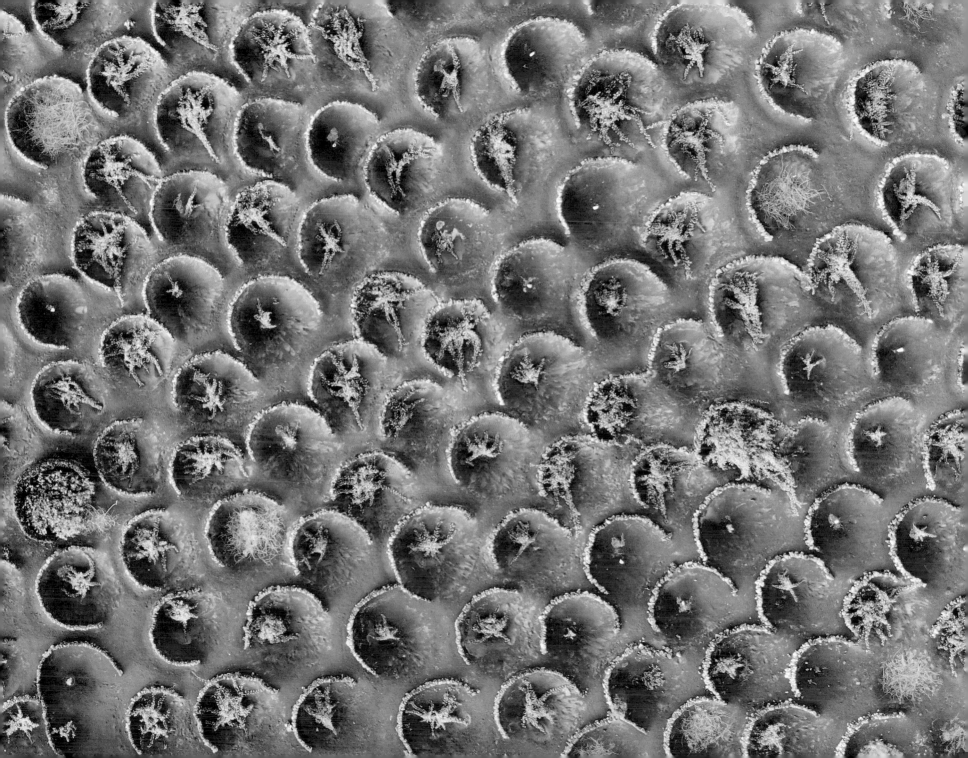

Above **Jardín de Cactus**, Guatiza; **Right Monumento al Campesino**, Mozaga

Blackened, twisted landscapes may not be the typical holiday-brochure centre-fold, but there's something satisfying about working a little to appreciate the unusual aesthetic of this island. And once you do, like César Manrique, you begin to see it not just as strikingly beautiful but as a vast open-air gallery.

The Natural Canvas

It's almost as though everyone here is inspired by the natural surroundings to make life just a little more beautiful. Take, for example, the island's wine-making re-gion, La Geria – with vines planted among the loose volcanic rock, the green leaves provide neat splashes of vibrancy against a monochrome backdrop. Instead of sitting in tethered rows, each vine is sunk into a hollow behind a low, semi-circular wall built, of course, from volcanic rock. The idyllic vineyards are perfectly placed and endlessly photogenic.

Lunar comparisons are rife on Lanzarote and never more so than in the Parque Na-cional de Timanfaya. Created by a volcanic eruption in 1730, the 51-sq-km park is a kaleidoscope of craters and barren peaks in hues of ochre, russet and deep grey. Like most attractions on the island, the park's restaurant was carefully created to fuse as much as possible into the ethereal surroundings – you can watch whatever meat you order sizzling on the all-natural, volcano-powered barbecue out back. It was designed, like so many things here, by César Manrique, the island's 'favourite son' and a talented, visionary architect.

César – Protector of an Island

Born in Arrecife in 1919, Manrique was the island's number one fan – and in

return, the inhabitants adore him to this day. After a spell of study in the US, he returned to Lanzarote in the 1960s, and having witnessed tourist resorts in other parts of Spain, instantly began to worry about *lanzaroteño* architecture following a similar pattern. Working with the local government, he made a lasting impact on the built aesthetics of the isle. The complete absence of high-rise hotels? That was him. The trademark uniform whitewashed houses with green or blue woodwork? Manrique's influence again.

Manrique was an esteemed artist as well as an architect, and working with local authorities on construction regulations was just one element of his grand plan for Lanzarote. He commenced creating an astounding collection of sculptures and architectural projects that not only avoided marring the landscape – but utilised it, merged with it and became part of the island's charm and top attractions.

Manrique Must-Sees

To understand Manrique and his work, a good starting point is the Fundación César Manrique. Created around a set of ancient volcanic bubbles and tunnels, this was the artist's home for two decades, becoming a gallery just before his death in 1992. Here you can see his grand vision at work – the smooth whitewashed walls and floors provide a remarkable contrast to the rocky volcanic canvas, but nothing has been bulldozed or altered to make way for the subterranean home. The space effortlessly combines artistic works by Picasso, Sempere and of course, paintings and drawings by Manrique himself, with vast picture windows displaying the natural landscape that inspired his work.

Far Left **Cacti**;
Left **El Diablo
sculpture by César
Manrique**, Parque
Nacional de Timanfaya;
Right **Jameos del Agua**

Manrique's masterpiece is largely considered to be the Jameos del Agua, another system of subterranean caves that he converted into a concert hall. The centrepiece is the cobalt blue lake, formed aeons ago as the nearby Atlantic flowed into the cave. Not to be confused with the white outdoor pool – a much-loved comfort added to the complex by Manrique.

A Lasting Legacy
In the tree-lined traditional village of Haría is the Casa Museo César Manrique – the home where the artist lived out his last days. As much shrine as museum, the house has been kept exactly as it was when Manrique was killed in a car accident, right down to the cluttered studio,

featuring an eerily half-completed canvas.

For some of his finished works, head to the Museo Internacional de Arte Comtemporàneo in Arrecife. Breathing fresh life into the 18th-century Castillo de San José building, the modern art collection sees Manrique's works adorn the walls alongside those of his contemporaries, including Joan Miró and Manolo Millares. In a lasting nod to Manrique's love of island panoramas, the restaurant below the gallery serves lavish lunches with a side order of marvellous views out to the Atlantic Ocean.

Perhaps the greatest homage to Manrique's influence is the opinions and devotion of the *lanzaroteños* themselves. The locals hold Manrique in the highest regard – he has a status close to saintliness

among the islanders, who credit his vision and deep love for Lanzarote as its saviour from the unsightly sky-high ravages of mass tourism. They recognise the island as his most important work of art and show their gratitude by continuing to protect and subtly magnify its other-worldly beauty.

To read about:
Córdoba's Patios in Bloom see page 106
Cabo de Gata see page 238

The Inland Beach: Playa de Gulpiyuri

More a sight than a sunbathing spot, this magical, 50m-long hidden cove framed by cliffs and greenery is one of Spain's most famous inland beaches. Located near Llanes in Asturias, this tiny beach could almost have been designed by a surrealist artist. Backed by majestic crags of limestone, it lies more than 100m from the sea shore. It's not a lake beach, nor an illusion: a tunnel beneath the rocks channels water from the Cantabrian Sea into a cove.

To read about:

Epic Rail Journeys: El Transcantábrico

As delicious and diverse as a local pintxo-bar spread, northern Spain's lusciously green landscapes look all the more spectacular from the comfort of the celebrated five-star Transcantábrico Clásico train. Jump on board for an eight-day, 1000km narrow-gauge adventure on one of Europe's earliest tourist-train triumphs – between Galicia's glittering Santiago de Compostela and majestic León, home to one of Spain's most exquisite cathedrals.

GALICIA JOURNEYS

Rolling partly along Spain's jagged northern coastline, from Santiago de Compostela to León, via Oviedo, Santander and Bilbao, and traversing five distinct autonomous communities, the much-romanticised, three-decades-old Transcantábrico is Spain's original tourist train. Its trundling route – past cascading cliffs, tucked-away golden coves, awe-inspiring viaducts, the rugged Picos de Europa, and villages sprinkled with *indiano* mansions – is rooted in the travels of the *hullero* train that brought coal to Bilbao's booming steel industry for over half a century, and whose journeys were vividly documented by Spanish writer Juan Pedro Aparicio in his 1982 work *El Transcantábrico*.

The initial section from Santiago to Ferrol happens, rather unromantically, by bus, but before you know it you're clinking glasses and swigging cider as the train pootles eastwards, leaving behind Galicia's craggy coastline and venturing towards Asturias' heaven-reaching peaks then Cantabria's loping green hills. On day four, you breakfast on board in low-key Arriondas and visit the Asturian Picos' shimmering Lago Enol and revered Santuario de Covadonga by bus, before winding north through the Río Sella gorge to dine in lively Llanes overlooking the Bay of Biscay. Other standout stops include Asturian capital Oviedo (with its unique Pre-Romanesque churches), Galicia's beautiful Praia As Catedrais, the architectural feast of Bilbao's Museo Guggenheim, and Cantabria's Unesco-listed Cueva de Altamira (home to some of the world's oldest cave art), just outside the pristine medieval village of Santillana del Mar – not to mention León's show-stopping 13th-century Gothic cathedral.

The food is exceptional: some meals (usually breakfast) are served on board but most are at carefully selected restaurants en route – so you get to sample, say, hearty Asturian *fabada* (a bean-and-meat stew), bite-sized Basque *pintxos* and superbly fresh Cantabrian seafood in one foodie-dream swoop. The train doesn't travel at night, meaning it's easy to sleep aboard and, in true Spanish style, stay out into the night.

The trip can also be done in reverse, from León to Santiago, or in smaller chunks with a four-day minimum. Meanwhile, the uber-high-end Transcantábrico Gran Lujo chugs its way along mostly the same tracks but cuts out the inland section to/from León in exchange for continuing east, following the coast to food-savvy San Sebastián in the Basque Country.

To read about:

Cantabria's Prehistoric Cave Art see page 156
Cycling the Railways of Andalucía see page 192

Sierra Nevada: Hiking Las Alpujarras

ANDALUCÍA HIKING

The Camino de Santiago might be Spain's most revered long-distance footpath, but with over a quarter of a million walkers now tackling the trek annually, it's hardly off the beaten track. For a more tranquil experience, decamp instead to the GR7, southern Spain's less-trodden camino, where you can roam alone above wispy clouds before descending for quiet nights in pilgrim-free villages.

Right **Bubión**

Of the many sections of Spain's *gran recorridos* (great tours) that are do-able in a week, few are as wondrous or user-friendly as the passage across the southern flank of Andalucía's Sierra Nevada and through the canyons and white villages of Las Alpujarras.

The magnetism of Las Alpujarras – aside from the monolithic mountain scenery – lies in the region's unusual Islamic heritage. This was the last refuge of the Moors in Spain. Long after Boabdil, Granada's final Nasrid sultan, capitulated to the Catholic monarchs in 1492, rebellious Moors were still waging a guerrilla war from isolated mountain bases in Las Alpujarras until as late as 1571. The lingering Moorish influence is reflected in the region's exotic place names, traditional artisan crafts and flat-roofed, Moroccan-style villages that lie splattered across steep-sided canyons like white cubes on a Picasso canvas.

The Path from Válor

The region's villages are linked by a thorough network of roads, but car-reliant travellers will only glean a fraction of what the Alpujarras are all about. Válor, close to the border with Almería province, is an ideal place to begin your journey and get culturally acquainted.

For a decent four- to five-day traverse of the Sierra Nevada's lower slopes, plan to head west out of Válor with the goal of reaching Lanjarón 82km away. Accommodation is easy to procure in the villages en route: Bérchules, Trevélez, Pitres and Capileira all have a fine selection of hotels and or guesthouses with no village ever more than 10km from the next. Most settlements are endowed with a restaurant, shop and

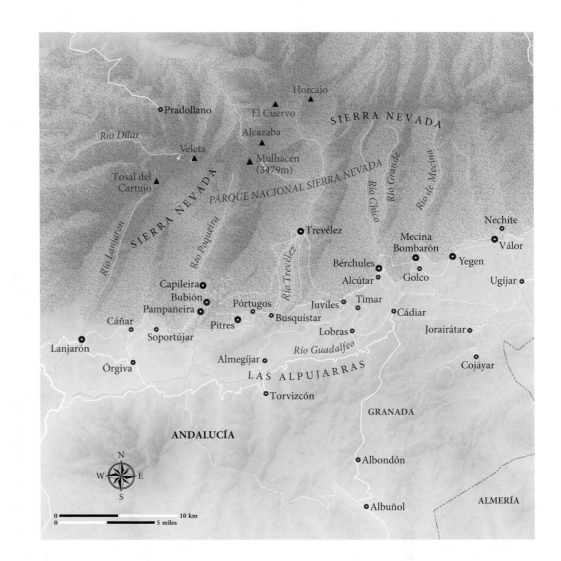

ancient communal fountain for refilling water bottles. Take a good map and learn to ask the way in Spanish (local farmers are rarely bilingual).

Pastures, Farmsteads & Olive Groves

The first main village west of Válor is Yegen, the one-time home of the British author and expat Gerald Brenan, who wrote about his isolated Andalucian life in the 1920s in the travelogue *South from Granada*. Brenan is fondly remembered in the town; his former house is furnished with a plaque and a local 2km walking route is named after him.

Further on is wonderfully bucolic Mecina Bombarón where you're more likely to get caught in a goat-jam than a traffic-jam. This part of the route, as it passes pastures, ruined farmsteads and olive groves, follows the erstwhile *camino real,* a one-time royal path between Granada and Almería. A medieval bridge on the eastern edge of Mecina stands as a historical marker.

Over the next 20km the villages get ever more spectacular until Trevélez, the second-highest village in Spain, which clings precipitously to an eponymous canyon in the shadow of Mulhacén, mainland Spain's highest peak.

The village can be used as a base to tackle the relatively easy hike up Mulhacén, but, if you're well and truly knackered by this point, it's also a good place to get on a bus and jump-cut to the Poqueira canyon further west. Trevélez is famous for its *jamón serrano* – cured ham that matures perfectly in the fresh mountain air. The hams hang ubiquitously on hooks in bars and shops around town, just out of head-butting distance.

Far left **Capileira**;
Left **Lanjarón**;
Right **Bubión**

From the arid, treeless landscapes of Trevélez your route swings on before dipping into La Tahá, a gentle, pastoral valley sprinkled with seven tightly knotted hamlets. The next canyon, the Barranco de Poqueira, five steep-ish kilometres away, is a busier option.

Fiestas & Artisan Workshops
Across a high ridge, the Barranco de Poqueira guards Pampaneira, Bubión and Capileira, Las Alpujarras' three prettiest and most quintessential villages, which sit stacked up on top of one another on steep, terraced slopes. Sharing a common Moorish heritage, the settlements are known for their feisty summer fiestas and traditional artisan workshops. You can while away countless hours watching leather makers, potters, loom operators and basket weavers religiously practicing their ancient crafts. This is possibly Spain's finest (and highest) spot for quality hand-made goods.

The only problem if you're hiking is that it's still 25km along sinuous paths to Lanjarón, not ideal if you're dragging a bag loaded with leather jackets, delicate ceramic pots and heavy Pampaneira blankets.

Hikers pressing on to Lanjarón should look out for golden and Bonelli's eagles as they approach their final destination. This 'gateway to the Alpujarras' is also notable for its cured ham, spring water and recuperative spa, all three of which could come in handy as you descend into town after five days of Alpujarran knee-bashing.

To read about:
Camino de Santiago Pilgrimage see page 42
White Villages of Andalucía see page 110

Kitesurfing: Costa de la Luz

ANDALUCÍA KITESURFING

Take to Andalucía's Atlantic waves in Europe's laid-back kitesurfing capital, Tarifa, backed by panoramas of Morocco looming across the Strait of Gibraltar and the beautiful blonde sands and evocative white-clad villages of Cádiz province's wind-blown Costa de la Luz. After, refuel with gloriously fresh seafood and glasses of fino *(dry sherry).*

Poised on Spain's southernmost tip, where the Mediterranean Sea folds into the Atlantic Ocean, ancient Tarifa is battered by winds so strong, relentless and legendary that the town's once-high suicide rate was rumoured to be the result of them driving people mad. While this may or may not be true, there's no denying that this small Costa de la Luz settlement – with its whitewashed old town, Moorish-origin castle, distinctly North African air and 10km of dreamy white-gold beaches – has morphed into Europe's premier windsurfing and kitesurfing destination.

Spurred on by the local *levante* and *poniente* winds, windsurfing landed in Tarifa in the 1970s, before being upstaged by its more fashionable younger sibling, kitesurfing, in the 1990s. Modern-day Tarifa is crammed with kitesurfing and windsurfing schools, which, combined with its sociable, international wave-riding crowd, tangible Moorish heritage and mostly Spanish holidaymakers, make this beachy enclave quite unlike any other in Andalucía.

The most popular kitesurfing and windsurfing strip is along the coast between Tarifa and the salt-white sand dune at Punta Paloma, taking in silky Los Lances and Valdevaqueros beaches. The best months to get to grips with these adrenalin-addled sports are May, June and September, though the Costa de la Luz' choppy seas aren't always beginners' territory.

But it isn't all just about wave-skimming sails and kites here. Sweeping northwest, past alternative, nudist-loved Los Caños de Meca (where rainbows of kites sparkle off powdery beaches surrounding the famous Cabo de Trafalgar), you arrive at mellow, golden-sand El Palmar, washed from October to May by Andalucía's finest board-surfing waves and easily enjoyed from the enchanting white town of Vejer de la Frontera.

Where to Learn

Tarifa alone is home to more than 30 multilingual schools offering gear hire and classes, from beginner to expert level, and there are more dotted along Cádiz' Costa de la Luz.

Gisela Pulido Pro Center This highly rated Tarifa-based kitesurfing school is led by world champion Gisela Pulido.

ION Club A respected windsurfing and kitesurfing specialist, with beginner, intermediate and advanced classes, as well as SUP (stand-up paddleboarding), it's located just northwest of Tarifa.

Escuela de Surf 9 Pies In surf-mad El Palmar, professional 9 Pies has surf classes and board hire for all levels, plus yoga and SUP.

To read about:
¡Olé! Fiery Flamenco see page 28
Spanish Sands see page 78

A Catalan Food Trail

Between the shining stars of Barcelona and Girona, rural Catalonia is an enthralling gourmet destination. This three-day trail starts in Barcelona but focuses on small-town Catalonia. It holds the promise of bulging botifarra (sausage), rich mountain cheese and lovingly seared vegetables, and takes you from the fresh seafood of the coast to the robust flavours of Catalonia's volcanic landscape.

Right **Coca de recapte**, a typical Catalan savoury flatbread

Landscape and history find rich expression on the Catalan plate. This fiercely distinct region of Spain encompasses an astonishing range of landscapes, from the sun-kissed Costa Brava to the Pyrenees, where lonely Romanesque monasteries are perched in wild valleys. *Mar i muntanya* (sea and mountain) dishes reflect the opposing extremes of Catalonia's terrain, uniting produce scooped from the coast with meat farmed in Pyrenean pastures. Bright flavours such as tomato and capsicum are omnipresent, their tang complemented by fragrant nuances of almond and dried fruit: legacies of Muslim rule in the Iberian Peninsula from the 7th century. The best dishes marry tart flavours with earthy notes to wondrous effect.

Catalan cuisine rose to global stardom in 2016 when the area was crowned European Region of Gastronomy. But some gastronomic enclaves remain relatively unknown outside Spain, such as La Garrotxa with its *cuina volcànica* (volcanic cuisine). Here in this bucolic area of the Catalan Pyrenees, hills and valleys have been sculpted by volcanoes that now slumber. The fertile, ashy soil is credited for the quality of local produce: turnips, truffles and chestnuts add depth to pork, while nut and herb liqueurs moisten the palate between forkfuls. Dishes are awarded a *cuina volcànica* mark to indicate locally sourced status and inventive use of traditional ingredients.

Mercat de la Boqueria

Begin your journey in Barcelona with an amuse-bouche of Catalan flavours at historic food hall La Boqueria. A market has stood here since the 13th century, though the hall housing it today is a mere

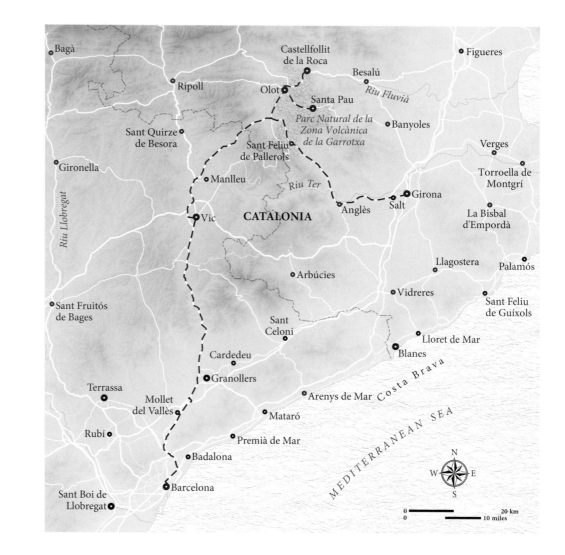

160 years young. The market is beloved by visitors, and you'll understand why with your first glance at produce ranging from grab-and-go *cargols* (snails) to slabs of goat's cheese and glistening cured meats

Follow local rhythms to find the best food: tourists tend to cluster at the main entrance, so don't get distracted by the rainbow of smoothie stalls. Find more elbow room (and local shoppers) by ploughing into the further realms of the market. Arrive early, as La Boqueria is hugely popular with tour groups, and don't miss taking away some *jamón ibérico* – rather than grabbing a package, find a vendor shaving off melt-in-mouth slices of this protected-status ham on demand.

The market's Pinotxo Bar is wildly popular, with local legend Juanito Bayen among the friendly crew dishing up plates of stewed chickpeas, washed down with generous glasses of wine. As you're by the Balearic Sea, sample fresh mussels, razor clams and *xipirons amb mongetes* (squid with beans).

Casa Riera Ordeix

Leaving Barcelona, head for the spirited town of Vic, about an hour's drive north. Among its labyrinthine old-town streets, you won't fail to notice weighty truncheons of meat hanging in deli windows. This treasured delicacy is *llonganissa*, first mentioned in the 14th century, gilded with protected status, and only produced in and around Vic.

Delve into centuries of *llonganissa* history at Casa Riera Ordeix, a factory with attached deli and one of only a handful of authorised local producers. Its experienced sausage makers trust the old

Above Fig and foie-gras dish, El Celler de Can Roca

methods, which you can find out about on an hour-long tour behind the scenes.

Pere, who has been making *llonganisses* for an impressive 32 years, explains that carefully chosen meat is mixed with diced bacon, sea salt and black pepper. The mixture is allowed to rest for a weekend and then packed into a natural casing, tied with twine and hung to dry for three to six months. The result is a glistening cured meat that makes your mouth water with every bite (and there'll be many – this chewy sausage is a workout for your jaw). Maribel, another factory worker who has hand-wrapped *llonganissa* sausages for a grand total of 29 years, finds them delicious with sugar and quality Champagne, a mouth-watering mix of salty and sweet.

Restaurant El Jardinet

Appetite whetted, sit down for a feast in the heart of medieval Vic. Restaurant El Jardinet serves some of the best regional dishes in a charming setting (including a terrace for sunny days).

Tuck into *fideuà,* fine wheat noodles strewn with seafood, or juicy *ibérico* pork, lightly braised. If you feel inspired by the peaceful garden, you're in good company – the locally loved 20th-century 'Prince of Catalan Poets', Josep Carner, spent time here.

Can Xel

The terrain begins to ripple with valleys and triangular hills on the approach to La Garrotxa's volcanic region, a 45-minute drive north from Vic. This fertile area is the heartland of *cuina volcànica,* famed for its full-bodied flavours.

Your first stop is in Santa Pau: a tiny village famous for its *fesol* (plump white beans), cherished by local chefs because of the way they absorb flavour while retaining their shape.

The best spot to try them is Can Xel. Order a plateful of *botifarra amb fesols de Santa Pau,* in which the beans accompany a succulent Catalan sausage with serious pedigree: *botifarra* dates almost to Roman times, with its recipe of lightly spiced pork little changed since then.

Museu de l'Embotit

Next, bite off a hunk of sausage history in the village of Castellfollit de la Roca, a 20-minute drive north of Santa Pau, in the northern part of the volcanic zone. For more than 20 years, this pint-size museum, based on the premises of local cured meat experts J Sala Riera, has been laying bare the mysteries of medieval sausage making, with displays of stuffing tools from across the centuries, photographs of workers in the company's 150-year history, and opportunities to sample various meaty treats at the end.

The village, perched precariously on a basalt cliff, also offers spectacular views of the surrounding region.

Les Cols

Take the road back into Olot, a 15-minute drive, but detour to Les Cols before you reach the centre. Fina Puigdevall, the chef at this revered slow-food restaurant, is something of a culinary poet. Puigdevall aims to express the richness of the surrounding scenery through the finest produce grown in the volcanic soil, especially mushrooms, nuts and root vegetables.

Without exception, the results are inventive and delicious, such as Catalan classics *calçots* served tempura-style.

Robust vegetable flavours, a calling card of *cuina volcànica,* come through in ice creams flavoured with pumpkin, while La Garrotxa's very own black truffles add smokiness to cheeses and game. Finish with *ratafia,* a herbal liqueur made from macerated green nuts, another iconic product of La Garrotxa's volcanic soil.

Rocambolesc

Head south for your final stop, Girona. On the outskirts of this romantic city, the culinary legends at El Celler de Can Roca stir up sensational Catalan cuisine – the only snag is the 11-month waiting list. More accessible to casual gourmands is Rocambolesc, on the left bank of the Onyar in central Girona.

Rocambolesc is the dessert-focused brainchild of Jordi Roca, one of the three brothers behind three-Michelin-star El Celler. Roca dreamed of a dessert trolley trundling around Girona, but when the practicalities proved bothersome, he established this ice-cream place instead.

The experience feels both sophisticated and gleefully childlike. Ice-cream flavours include chocolate dark enough to blot out the sun, zesty strawberry, and violet, with up to 35 toppings to adorn each cloud-like serving.

Find space in your luggage for Rocambolesc's jars of sweets or a box of absurdly tall cupcakes, which tower with frosting, French-style macarons and chocolate baubles.

To read about:

Right Roasted *calçots* with romesco sauce

Fiesta of Fire: Las Fallas

The exuberant, anarchic swirl of the festival of Las Fallas de San José – fireworks, music, festive bonfires and all-night partying – is a must if you're visiting Spain in mid-March. While almost every pueblo (village) in the southeastern region has its own fiesta, it's at its most spectacular in the town of Valencia.

No one knows the exact origins of this loud, and we mean loud, festival, but the first written record dates from the second half of the 18th century. The *fallas* are huge sculptures of papier mâché on wood built by teams of local artists. Each neighbourhood sponsors its own *falla*, and on the morning of 16 March when the city wakes after the *plantà* (the overnight construction of the *fallas*), more than 350 have sprung up. Reaching up to 15m in height, with the most expensive costing hundreds of thousands of euros, these grotesque, colourful effigies satirise celebrities, current affairs and customs, ranging from comical to moving. It's a custom that grew through the 19th and 20th centuries and now has World Heritage status.

From 12 to 19 March, around-the-clock festivities include street parties, paella-cooking competitions, parades and open-air concerts. Las Fallas prides itself on its fireworks: each day at 2pm a *mascletà* (more than five minutes of deafening thumps and explosions) shakes the window panes of Plaza del Ayuntamiento.

After midnight on the final day each *falla* goes up in flames – *la cremà* (the burning) backed by yet more fireworks. A popular vote spares the most-cherished *ninot* (the figurines that pose at the base of each *falla*), which gets housed for posterity, and visiting, in the Museo Fallero.

Many locals dress in regional and historical costumes, and you can get into the spirit of the festival by visiting a shop such as Álvaro Moliner that sells traditional *valenciana* outfits.

To read about:

The Perfect Paella see page 84
Egg-splosive Flour War see page 210

The Unspoilt Mediterranean: Cabo de Gata

Spain's best-kept secret lies near the tourist-filled Costa del Sol – the undiscovered region of Almería, filled with national parks, unspoilt beaches and mesmerising desert.

ALMERÍA LANDSCAPES

Love, honour and revenge – the dark, clashing passions of old Spain – come together in an imposing farmhouse set against the austere volcanic backdrop of Cabo de Gata. Here, in the forgotten part of Spain that is Almería, is the scene of an honour killing which inspired one of the country's great pieces of literature, playwright Federico García Lorca's *Blood Wedding*. Like so many things in this miraculously unblemished region in Spain's southeastern corner, it is completely deserted.

The whitewashed *cortijo,* with its peeling plaster and cock-eyed belltower, is a piece of petrified history. Inside, the roof is half down but there's no damp smell. Cabo de Gata is the driest place in Spain. Buildings here do not rot. They desiccate. This bare, cobwebbed chapel is where Casimiro Pérez was jilted at the altar by his fiancée, Francisca Cañada. She had run off that same morning with her secret lover, Paco Montes. Casimiro's family sought

instant revenge. They hunted the young couple down, wounding Francisca and killing her lover with three shots. It is one of the tragic stories of Spain. Lorca set his version in fertile Granada. Here, in the barren, rugged terrain of Almería, it makes more sense. For the dramatic beauty of Cabo de Gata derives from the same harsh elements that harden life itself.

In a remarkable Mediterranean wilderness, the Cabo de Gata natural park is shaped by the primitive forces of volcanoes and so starved of rain that it feels like a piece of Africa transported onto European soil. It is this uniqueness that Spain has decided to conserve. In a country whose coastline has been ravaged by developers, the survival of a vast stretch of unspoilt Mediterranean countryside is nothing more than a gift from the gods.

A dirt track leading away from the shack is lined with agaves and dwarf palms – the desert plants that do best in this arid land shaped by volcanic eruptions

and lava flows some eight million years ago. Three wire-haired sheepdogs chase up the stragglers. In the old days people cropped the palms and the thick esparto grass to make baskets, hats and sandals.

Over the last few decades, Spain's Mediterranean paradises have been despoiled by humans and concrete mixers. The carpet of bricks and cement has extended like two dark stains along both the south and east coasts. This park, with its 65km of protected coastline, stops them joining up. A remote retreat, Almería is *'el culo de España'* (the arse of Spain), according to locals. People used to say it was closer to London than Madrid. At least you could get there by ship. That is exactly what has saved it. It was too far from motorways, airports and electricity lines for early developers to bother with. Water was scarce and sewage systems nonexistent in the tiny villages. When Cabo de Gata became a natural park in 1987, most roads were still dirt tracks.

Above La Isleta del Moro; Right Tabernas Desert

The view from the cliffs at Amatista is of a placid, turquoise sea and ranks of basalt promontories, beaches and coves. For once, there is not a building, not even a boat, in sight. This is the raw Mediterranean of the romantic writers who marvelled at a country untouched by progress in the 19th and early 20th centuries.

At sundown in the village of Cabo de Gata two men row in from their small fishing boat. They winch the rowboat up onto a beach and carry a single bucket that's only half-full, with scad, mackerel, red mullet, dogfish and a single starfish. If distance has kept Cabo de Gata pure, the whims of one local landowning family have also been key. José González Montoya, who died in 1976, simply never wanted to sell. His family still owns 3000 hectares of parkland but has stayed faithful to his vision of slow, gradual development at one with its surroundings.

A wide, bumpy gravel track leads out of San José past the virgin beaches – Los Genoveses, Monsul, La Cala de la Media Luna – that old González refused to build on. These are names that locals, aware of how unique they are, utter with reverence. Fields of cereals dotted with poppies and plantations of agave and *chumberas* – the prickly pear cactus – stretch down the sloping basin of the Bay of the Genoveses to the beach.

Desert Gold

Almería is a place of extremes. Its landscapes, seemingly in constant battle with the elements, impress by scale and severity. Nowhere is this more apparent than in the Tabernas Desert, a natural park 40km inland from Cabo de Gata. The relentless barrenness of Europe's only true desert

is a place that may never need protection from people. For people, on the whole, have been too scared to venture into it.

With its wide open spaces, Almería is one of the world's great film sets. Peter O'Toole strode across Monsul beach in *Lawrence of Arabia* – one of hundreds of films shot around Cabo de Gata and in the extraordinary deserts of Almería's interior.

When Europe's film-makers want a landscape to rival the deserts of Arizona or the Mojave, this is where they come – to a place where it rains just four days a year and temperatures soar to 48°C (118°F) in the shade, if you can find any. It is not difficult to see why Sergio Leone brought Clint Eastwood and Lee Van Cleef to these parts to make classic spaghetti westerns like *The Good, The Bad and The Ugly*. Even scientists refer to these as badlands – uninhabitable and, for farming, beyond the scope of human ingenuity. A track cuts through the scrub, past a circle of tepees and into the permanent film set that is Fort Bravo. A horse gallops past, charging towards a stockade where other horses await. A cloud of dust obscures the wooden buildings – from a fortified bank to a Mexican cantina – of the empty set.

To read about:

Spanish Cinema see page 174
Kitesurfing: Costa de la Luz see page 228

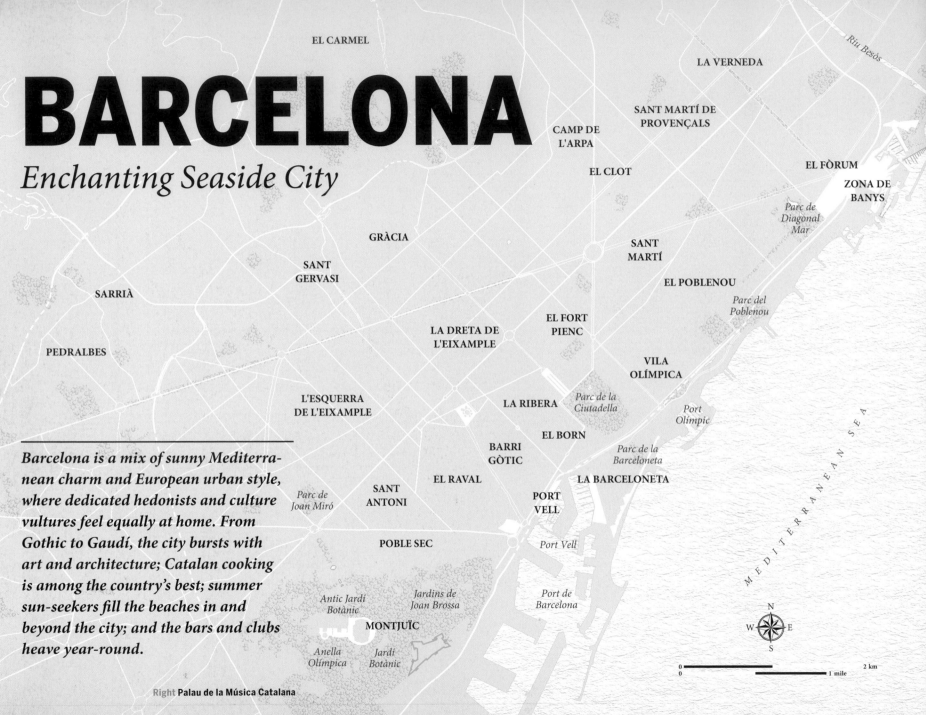

BARCELONA
Enchanting Seaside City

Barcelona is a mix of sunny Mediterranean charm and European urban style, where dedicated hedonists and culture vultures feel equally at home. From Gothic to Gaudí, the city bursts with art and architecture; Catalan cooking is among the country's best; summer sun-seekers fill the beaches in and beyond the city; and the bars and clubs heave year-round.

Right Palau de la Música Catalana

EL CARMEL

LA VERNEDA

SANT MARTÍ DE PROVENÇALS

CAMP DE L'ARPA

EL CLOT

EL FÒRUM

ZONA DE BANYS

Riu Besòs

Parc de Diagonal Mar

GRÀCIA

SANT MARTÍ

SANT GERVASI

EL POBLENOU

SARRIÀ

Parc del Poblenou

PEDRALBES

LA DRETA DE L'EIXAMPLE

EL FORT PIENC

VILA OLÍMPICA

L'ESQUERRA DE L'EIXAMPLE

LA RIBERA

Parc de la Ciutadella

Port Olímpic

EL BORN

Parc de la Barceloneta

BARRI GÒTIC

EL RAVAL

LA BARCELONETA

Parc de Joan Miró

SANT ANTONI

PORT VELL

POBLE SEC

Port Vell

Port de Barcelona

Antic Jardí Botànic

Jardins de Joan Brossa

MONTJUÏC

MEDITERRANEAN SEA

Anella Olímpica

Jardí Botànic

N
W E
S

0 ──────── 2 km
0 ──────── 1 mile

THE GENIUS OF GAUDÍ

At the end of the 19th century, Barcelona's prosperity unleashed one of the most imaginative periods in Spanish architecture. The architects at work here, who drew on prevailing art-nouveau trends as well as earlier Spanish styles, came to be called the Modernistas. Chief among them, Antoni Gaudí sprinkled Barcelona with jewels of his singular imagination.

Right **The apse**, La Sagrada Família

In the 1850s a rapidly growing city fuelled by industrialisation meant notoriously crowded conditions in the narrow streets of the Ciutat Vella, Barcelona's old quarter. It was time to break down the medieval walls and dramatically expand the city. In 1869 architect Ildefons Cerdà was chosen to design a new district, which would be called L'Eixample (the Expansion).

He drew wide boulevards on a gridlike layout, and envisioned neighbourhoods with plenty of green space – an objective that city planners unfortunately overruled amid the rampant land speculation of the day. With a blank slate before them, and abundant interest from upper-class residents eager to custom-design a new home, architects were much in demand. What developers could not have predicted was the calibre of those architects.

Early Days

Born in Reus and initially trained in metal-work, Antoni Gaudí i Cornet (1852–1926) personifies, and largely transcends, the Modernisme movement. In childhood he suffered from poor health, including rheumatism, and became an early adopter of a vegetarian diet. He was not a promising student. In 1878, when he obtained his architecture degree, the school's headmaster is reputed to have said, 'Who knows if we have given a diploma to a nutcase or a genius. Time will tell.'

As a young man, what most delighted Gaudí was being outdoors, and he became fascinated with plants, animals and geology. This deep admiration for the natural world would heavily influence his designs. 'This tree is my teacher,' he once said. 'Everything comes from the book of nature.' Throughout his work,

Gaudí sought to emulate the harmony he observed in the natural world, eschewing the straight line and favouring curvaceous forms and more organic shapes.

The spiral of a nautilus shell can be seen in staircases and ceiling details, tight buds of flowers in chimney pots and roof ornamentation; undulating arches evoke a cavern, overlapping roof tiles mimic the scales of an armadillo and flowing walls resemble waves on the sea. Tree branches, spider webs, stalactites, honeycombs, starfish, mushrooms, shimmering beetle wings and many other elements from nature were all part of the Gaudían vernacular, and he took pride in using the building materials of the countryside: clay, stone and wood.

Gaudí was also a devout Catholic and a Catalan nationalist, and his creations were a conscious expression of Catalan identity and, in some cases, of great piety. Gaudí's structural approach owed much to the austere era of Catalan Gothic, which inspired his own inventive work with parabolic arches.

Gaudí Creations
La Sagrada Família

Gaudí's masterpiece and all-consuming obsession was La Sagrada Família (begun in 1882), and in it you can see the culminating vision of many ideas developed over the years. Its massive scale evokes the grandeur of Catalonia's Gothic cathedrals, while organic elements foreground its harmony with nature.

Commissioned by a conservative society that wished to build a temple as atonement for the city's sins of modernity, the church is rife with symbols that tangibly express Gaudí's Catholic faith through

Key Features of Modernista Buildings

For many, Modernisme is synonymous with Gaudí, but he was by no means alone. Lluís Domènech i Montaner and Josep Puig i Cadafalch left a wealth of remarkable buildings across the city, while the Rome-trained sculptor Eusebi Arnau was one of the most popular figures called upon to decorate Barcelona's Modernista piles. Alongside Gaudí, these architects and artists looked to the past for inspiration. Gothic, Islamic and Renaissance design all had something to offer. At its most playful, Modernisme was able to intelligently flout the rule books of these styles and forge exciting new creations. When strolling Barcelona's streets, keep an eye out for Modernisme's flamboyant designs and tell-tale structural devices:

→ Parabolic arches
→ Organic shapes (bones, branches, leaves, nautilus shells)
→ Fanciful chimney pots
→ Colourful, shimmering tiles
→ Budlike, cone-shaped towers
→ Mosaic-covered surfaces
→ Sculptural details of flora and fauna
→ Treelike columns
→ Exquisite details (stained glass, wrought iron, ceramics)
→ Playful historical references (dragons for Catalan patron saint, St George; Gothic-style carvings for Barcelona's medieval past)

Left **Nativity Facade**, La Sagrada Família

architecture: 18 bell towers symbolise Jesus, the Virgin Mary, the four evangelists and the 12 apostles. Three facades cover Jesus's life, death and resurrection. Even its location is relevant: the Nativity Facade faces east where the sun rises; the Passion Facade depicting Christ's death faces west where the sun sets.

At Gaudí's death, only the crypt, the apse walls, one portal and one tower had been finished. Three more towers were added by 1930, completing the northeast (Nativity) facade. In 1936 anarchists burned and smashed the interior, including workshops, plans and models. Work began again in 1952 and still continues today, but controversy has always clouded progress. Opponents of the continuation of the project claim that the computer models based on what little of Gaudí's plans survived the anarchists' ire have led to the creation of a monster that has little to do with Gaudí's intentions.

Palau Güell
Gaudí seems to have particularly enjoyed himself with rooftops. At Palau Güell he created all sorts of fantastical, multicoloured tile figures as chimney pots resembling oversized budlike trees that seem straight out of Alice in Wonderland – or perhaps Dr Seuss. Gaudí built the palace just off La Rambla in the late 1880s for his wealthy and faithful patron, the industrialist Count Eusebi Güell. Although a little sombre compared with some of his later whims, it is still a characteristic riot of styles (Gothic, Islamic, art nouveau) and materials.

Park Güell
Unesco-listed Park Güell is where Gaudí turned his hand to landscape gardening.

The park was created in 1900, when Eusebi Güell bought a tree-covered hillside (then outside Barcelona) and hired Gaudí to create a miniature city of houses for the wealthy in landscaped grounds. The project was a commercial flop and was abandoned in 1914 – but not before Gaudí had created 3km of roads and walks, steps, a plaza and two gatehouses in his inimitable manner. In 1922 the city bought the estate for use as a public park. The best views are from the cross-topped Turó del Calvari in the southwest corner.

Casa Batlló
Gaudí's work is an earthy appeal to sinewy movement, but often with a dreamlike or surreal quality. The private apartment block Casa Batlló, remodelled by Gaudí in 1904, is a fine example in which all appears a riot of the unnaturally natural – or the naturally unnatural. Not only are straight lines eliminated, but the lines between real and unreal, sober and dream-drunk, good sense and play are all blurred. This is Gaudí at his hallucinatory best. The facade, sprinkled with bits of blue, mauve and green tiles, and studded with wave-shaped window frames and balconies, rises to an uneven blue-tiled roof with a solitary tower. Depending on how you look at the facade, you might see St George (the patron saint of Catalonia) defeating a dragon, a magnificent and shimmering fish (a symbol of Mediterranean peoples) or elements of an effusive Carnaval parade.

La Pedrera
This madcap Gaudí masterpiece was built in 1905–10 as a combined apartment and office block. Formally called Casa Milà, after the businessman who commissioned it, it is better known as La Pedrera (the Quarry) because of its uneven grey stone facade, which ripples around the corner of Carrer de Provença, evoking a cliff-face sculpted by waves and wind. The wave effect is emphasised by elaborate wrought-iron balconies that bring to mind seaweed washed up on the shore. The lasting impression is of a building on the verge of motion.

To read about:
Guggenheim: The Bilbao Effect see page 168
Barcelona Beyond the Crowds see page 250

BARCELONA BEYOND THE CROWDS

BARCELONA PEOPLE & CULTURE

Barcelona's popularity as a tourist destination has surged in recent years, but there are still many local barrios (districts) to explore away from the crowds. In the centre you'll be jostling for space among tour groups, bicycles and selfie sticks; visit these neighbourhoods, though, and you might be one of the few there. Explore vast empty parks, visit Gaudí buildings where you won't have to queue, admire spectacular city views, and get to know areas of the city even many locals don't know.

Right **Parc del Laberint d'Horta**

Sant Andreu de Palomar

The village-like *barrio* of Sant Andreu de Palomar lies to the northeast of Barcelona's centre, and is one of the most charming in the city. In fact, it used to be an independent village until it merged with the city in the late 1800s. Even locals don't know this *barrio*, unless they live there.

Despite not being well-known, Sant Andreu has some intriguing sights. At the heart sits the Plaza Orfila, and the striking Church of Sant Andreu, one of the most unusual in the city. Built on the site of a 10th-century Romanesque church, it's neo-Gothic in style and has become a symbol of the *barrio*.

The neighbourhood is filled with quaint squares, lots of independent shops and cafes, and mesmerising Modernista architecture. Stop by the Sant Andreu covered market, one of the most traditional in Barcelona. In the cobbled streets behind the market, you'll find the Parròquia de Sant Pacià, another lovely neo-Gothic church with ribbed vaults, and original tiles designed by none other than Antoni Gaudí.

Horta

The quaint, quiet *barrio* of Horta lies to the north of the centre and west of Sant Andreu, and brims with cute plazas and narrow streets. Other than sitting down with the locals to enjoy a nice cold *orxata* (tiger nut milk) or two in a pretty square, your main reason for coming here will be the Parc del Laberint d'Horta – a huge green expanse that sits high up among rolling hills. Dating to the late 1700s and early 1800s, it's the oldest garden in Barcelona and is both neoclassical and Romantic in style. Today, the spot has been caught and consumed by the city's voracious suburbs, enveloped by apartment buildings and ring roads. Its status as an oasis is all the more prized as a result. Filled with graceful pavilions, ponds, waterfalls, and busts and statues inspired by Greek and Roman mythology, its highlight is a huge central labyrinth – a proper cypress hedge maze you can really get lost in.

El Carmel

The neighbourhood of El Carmel sits just below Horta, and above Gaudí's famous Park Güell. While almost all tourists visit Park Güell, few venture further. El Carmel is characterised by steep narrow streets and leafy residential areas; there aren't many sights, but the neighbourhood more than makes up for that by offering some incredible city views. You'll need to be fit to walk the hilly streets of El Carmel, and even fitter still to climb to the top of Turó de la Rovira to visit the Bunkers del Carmel. Built during the Spanish Civil War, the bunkers were used to house anti-aircraft guns, but later during the 1940s to 1960s they became something of a shanty town. Today, locals, students and expats gather here at sunset with picnics and guitars, but if you can wake up early enough, sunrise is even better. It's from up here that you can enjoy the best view in the whole of Barcelona – a panoramic snapshot of the city that lets you pick out its most iconic landmarks.

Sarrià

Sarrià is Barcelona's upmarket *barrio* for the well-heeled, filled with luxury apartments, quiet narrow streets, picturesque squares and elegant Catalan architecture. Sarrià, like Sant Andreu, used to be a separate village until it was swallowed up by the city. It was in fact the last village to annex to Barcelona, doing so in the latter half of the 19th century.

The *barrio*'s most fascinating sight is one of Gaudí's lesser-known buildings – the Bellesguard tower. This masterpiece was rescued from obscurity and opened to the public in 2013. Built between 1900 and 1909, this private residence (still owned by the original Guilera family) has a castle-like appearance with crenellated walls of stone and brick, narrow stained-glass windows, elaborate ironwork and a soaring turret mounted by a Gaudían cross. It's a fascinating work that combines both Gothic and Modernista elements.

Pedralbes

The Pedralbes *barrio* sits to the west of Sarrià, and is characterised by wide leafy avenues and graceful mansions, backed by the green hills of the Collserola natural park. Make a stop at the Pavellons Güell, fronted by Gaudí's exquisite Dragon Gate with its intricate curls of wrought iron.

At the top of Avinguda Pedralbes, you'll find the Monastir de Pedralbes, hidden behind a stone arch down a narrow cobbled street. Founded in 1327, it features a fresco-covered chapel and arched cloisters surrounding a garden-like courtyard. Further west, along Avinguda Diagonal, you'll come to the Palau de Pedralbes, painted yellow and covered in rose-coloured stencils; built in the 1900s, it was once the home of the Spanish royal family when they visited Barcelona. The last stop along the avenue is the Parc de Cervantes, filled with over 240 varieties of rose, including the world's most fragrant – the Mister Lincoln, a hybrid tea rose.

To read about:
Game of Thrones on Location see page 176
The Holiday Season in Barcelona see page 260

FC BARCELONA: MORE THAN A CLUB

One of the great football powerhouses of today, FC Barcelona has always been 'més que un club' ('more than a club'). This motto, coined back in 1968, does a fine job evoking the deeper sense of Catalan identity that so many barcelonins feel when the blaugranes (blue and scarlet) take the field.

Camp Nou

A pilgrimage site for football fans from around the world, FC Barcelona's home stadium of Camp Nou is hallowed ground. The size is staggering – with a near 100,000-seat capacity, this is one of the largest football stadiums on earth – and during matches, the roar of the crowd is incredible. These days, Catalan pride runs high, with fans waving *banderas independentistas* (independence flags) and giving added resonance to the lines of the club anthem: '*Mai ningú no ens podrá tòrcer!*' ('We can never be defeated!').

While nothing compares to the excitement of attending a live match, the 'Camp Nou Experience' is a must for FC Barcelona fans. On this self-guided visit, you'll get an in-depth look at the club, starting with a museum filled with hands-on exhibitions, historical displays and trophies (Lionel Messi gets his own special area). All that's followed by a tour of the stadium. Diehard fans might feel a little weak in the knees after walking through the tunnel and on to the edge of the pitch. You'll also get to peek inside the visiting team's dressing room, the television studio, the press room and the commentary boxes.

The three-storey FC Botiga Megastore is also on the grounds. Here you'll find any piece of Barça's gear you can imagine, and customised jerseys with your name and preferred number, ready for you that same day.

Where to Watch a Game
La Taverna de Barcelona
Not your typical sports bar, this tavern channels a classy 1930s vibe, with dark wood furniture and old-fashioned photos of bygone days covering the panelled walls. Add to this a few well-placed screens and a throng of staunch FC Barcelona fans, and you have a memorable setting for catching the latest match of La Liga. There are also tapas, ever-flowing pitchers of sangría and live bands from time to time (on non-game nights of course). It's located right around the corner from Plaça de Catalunya, a short stroll from La Rambla.

Mau Mau Underground
A fine alternative to the tourist-filled pubs of the Barri Gòtic, Mau Mau Underground feels more like a lounge, with sofas and a stylish interior set in a former warehouse space in the neighbourhood of Poble Sec. Watching a game here – on one of the two giant screens – feels more like being in a private loft than in a bar. The drink of choice is gin, with more than 35 types on hand. It normally opens only Thursdays to Saturdays, and whenever there's a big FC Barcelona match happening.

La Pròrroga
In the youthful neighbourhood of Gràcia, this much-loved drinking den, whose name means 'Overtime' in Spanish, goes mad for Barça when the Catalan side takes the field. It draws a mostly local crowd and has a friendly, festive vibe. The setting is a bit of industrial chic with exposed bulbs, tall ceilings and a long wooden bar, where Barça fans watch in hushed silence while sipping frothy pints and nibbling on tapas. The beer selection is decent – and the self-service system is remarkably efficient. Go early to score a table, otherwise, plan on standing for the length of the match.

Curiosities & Historical Intrigue
Font de Canaletes
Near the Barri Gòtic, this elegant 19th-century drinking fountain is a favourite meeting spot for FC Barcelona supporters after major matches. Strategically placed near the northern end of La Rambla (the city's most famous pedestrian strip), the fountain has been drawing post-game fans since the 1930s – back in those days, the offices of the sporting newspaper *La Rambla* stood just opposite the fountain, and the paper would hang a blackboard announcing the results of the game outside the door. While you're here, go ahead and take a big swig out of one of the four water spouts. According to legend, whoever drinks from the fountain will come back to Barcelona.

Barça's Civil War Connections
As one of the last holdouts against Franco during the Spanish Civil War, Barcelona suffered heavily. FC Barcelona, which had become for many residents a rallying point for Catalan resistance against the central government, was particularly targeted. The club's president, Josep Sunyol, was on his way back to Barcelona after visiting Republican troops just days after the start of the war in 1936, when his chauffeured vehicle was stopped by Francoist forces, and he was summarily executed. A few years later, in March 1938, the FC Barcelona Social Club in L'Eixample district was bombed.

Nearby parts of the city still bear the scars from aerial raids. In the Barri Gòtic, the pockmarked walls around Plaça Sant Felip Neri show the devastation from one particularly gruesome day of bombard-

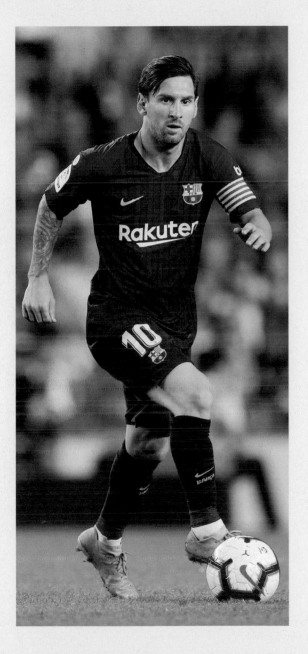

ment. *Barcelonins* dug air-raid shelters into the hills around the city for protection. Up on Montjuïc, you can visit a well-preserved shelter, known as Refugi 307, that provides a window into that harrowing time.

Relive Quini's Rescue

One of the most unusual events in FC Barça's history transpired a few blocks east of Camp Nou. In March 1981, famed striker Enrique 'Quini' Castro was kidnapped just after playing in a match against Hércules de Alicante (scoring two of the team's six goals). He was taken at gunpoint, thrown into the boot of a car and whisked away to an unknown location. When the story broke, journalists and police descended on the area, and Can Fusté, a restaurant below the footballer's apartment, became the base of police operations. Working round the clock, police managed to track down the criminals and free Quini – some 25 days after he was taken. The story ended well for Quini, though FC Barcelona played poorly without their star player, and lost any chance of the league title that year.

Some 35 years later, Can Fusté is still operating and makes a fine spot for dining on market-fresh Catalan cuisine while contemplating the past (as Quini did when he reunited here in 2012 with 10 of the policemen who helped free him).

RCD Espanyol: Barcelona's Other Club

Football in Barcelona has the aura of religion and for much of the city's population, support of FC Barcelona is an article of faith. But the city has another hardy (if less illustrious) side: RCD Espanyol. FC Barcelona is traditionally associated with the Catalans and even Catalan nationalism, while Espanyol is often identified with Spanish immigrants from other parts of the country.

To read about:

Kitesurfing: Costa de la Luz see page 228
Cycle the City see page 258

Left Camp Nou; **Above Lionel Messi**

DANCE OF THE DEVILS: FESTES DE LA MERCÈ

Barcelona's co-patron saint is celebrated with fervour during Festes de la Mercè (Festival of the Virgin of Mercy), a massive five-day festival. It is the Catalan capital's festa major and a final burst of prewinter madness. The city stages sporting events, free concerts, dance performances, and a fiery correfoc (fire run). The correfoc sees crowds hurl themselves along Via Laietana before 'devils', fire-spurting beasts and kids armed with firecrackers.

To read about:
¡Olé! Fiery Flamenco see page 28
The Holiday Season in Barcelona see page 260

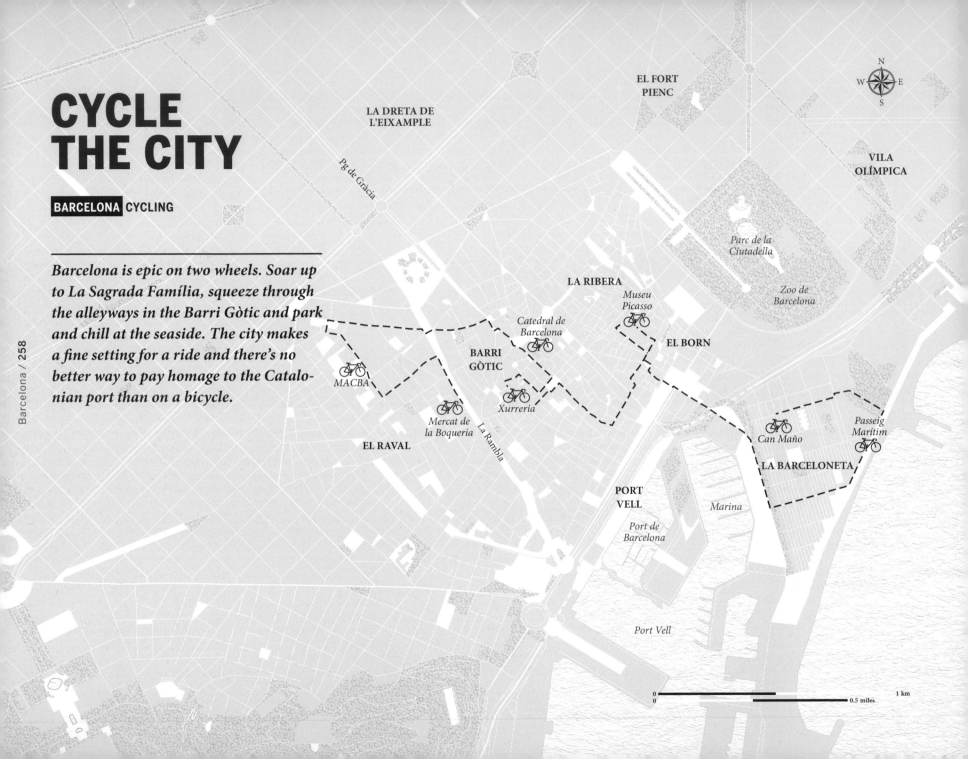

CYCLE THE CITY

BARCELONA CYCLING

Barcelona is epic on two wheels. Soar up to La Sagrada Família, squeeze through the alleyways in the Barri Gòtic and park and chill at the seaside. The city makes a fine setting for a ride and there's no better way to pay homage to the Catalonian port than on a bicycle.

LA DRETA DE L'EIXAMPLE

EL FORT PIENC

VILA OLÍMPICA

Pg de Gràcia

Parc de la Ciutadella

Zoo de Barcelona

LA RIBERA

Museu Picasso

EL BORN

Catedral de Barcelona

BARRI GÒTIC

MACBA

Xurreria

Mercat de la Boqueria

EL RAVAL

La Rambla

Can Maño

Passeig Marítim

LA BARCELONETA

PORT VELL

Marina

Port de Barcelona

Port Vell

0   0.5 miles   1 km

Sitting in Park Güell, on Gaudí's incredible serpentine mosaic bench, you'll look down at the panorama of Barcelona with the glittering Mediterranean beyond. Within 20 minutes, you're chewing pizza in the Barri Gòtic, and a short while later, eating ice cream on a baking beach.

And all of this can be done without stepping on a bus or a train, for Barcelona is becoming one of Europe's most cycle-friendly cities. Rent from one of its bicycle-hire shops and you'll soon be pedalling gingerly down those small, pedestrianised medieval streets, or in the summer sunshine of Barcelona's cycle-ways. Cycling in Barcelona particularly comes alive on Sundays, when a bike gives you the freedom of the city. Fuel up on a chocolate croissant at a cafe in the hip El Born district, before pedalling across Parc de la Ciutadella to Barcelona's old fishing quarter, La Barceloneta, to witness one of Europe's great weekly *paseos* (strolls). On one side the area has urban beach; on the other, the dramatic architecture for which the city is renowned; in between, you'll find yourself part of an endless stream of walkers, rollerbladers and cyclists.

In recent years, Barcelona's administration has done much to promote cycling. Good news, as there's something about the city's pace, the sunshine, the slow traffic, top restaurants and first-rate museums that works well on two wheels. Flanked by hills like Montjuïc (the fit are welcome to try), downtown Barcelona is mostly flat, an elegant mix of bisecting boulevards behind which run tangled medieval alleyways. There's a coastline, a few beaches, myriad sights and museums, tapas bars everywhere and the most vivid street life in Europe.

By bike you can cover the sights more rapidly – and have a great time doing so. As Barcelona visitor Ernest Hemingway once put it, 'you have no such accurate remembrance of country you have driven through as you gain by riding a bicycle'.

Barcelona has an increasing number of bicycle-hire shops offering bikes and anything remotely resembling one, from tandems to tricycle carts and more, as well as guided bike tours that take in sights like La Sagrada Família, La Barceloneta beach and Modernista buildings. Most start on La Rambla, the heart of the old city. This broad pedestrian boulevard carves a slice from Plaça de Catalunya and the early 20th-century L'Eixample district to the steamy docks and then to the beaches. Or go the other way along the Passeig de Gràcia boulevard – look out for Antoni Gaudí's Casa Batlló – leading to the elegant Gràcia district.

For a tour from La Rambla, dismount and stop at Mercat de la Boqueria, take a coffee at a bar, and then edge into El Raval, the district made infamous by Jean Genet in *A Thief's Journal* (1949). Although gentrifying with hip cafes, its picturesque alleyways can be rough, but on a bike you'll sail past the city's saltier characters. Here, visit MACBA, the Museum of Contemporary Art, and muse over avant-garde artworks. Crossing to the other side of La Rambla, cycle the Barri Gòtic towards the grand La Ribera district through a grid of medieval streets. Break out into the Plaça Nova to see the Catedral de Barcelona (known as La Seu), then stop at Xurreria for a hot chocolate and *churros* (Spanish doughnuts). Cycle on to take in the Museu Picasso, an exquisite display in a rambling old palace.

Bicing Barcelona

In 2007, Barcelona's City Council started Bicing, a bicycle-sharing scheme. It's available to locals only, so tourists have to hire, but the project has opened the city's eyes to cycling and encouraged many residents to take to two wheels. Meanwhile, Barcelona has opened up its streets, already pedestrian-friendly, to bicycles, with 180km of bike lanes and shared space with cars. There's even a 'Bicycle Counter' on Passeig de St Joan, setting out the goals for cycling in the city.

Freewheel down to La Barceloneta to hit Passeig Marítim – the seafront promenade and Barcelona's best ride. Later, pedal back to one of La Barceloneta's earthy restaurants for a *flauta* (tall glass) of beer and some fried octopus at Can Maño on Carrer del Baluard. Rich, yes – but earned.

To read about:
A Rock Climber's Paradise see page 208
The Genius of Gaudí see page 244

THE HOLIDAY SEASON IN BARCELONA

There are few places on earth as festive-feeling as Barcelona's chocolate-box medieval heart over the Christmas period (which here runs until Kings' Day, or Twelfth Night). Even the narrowest of alleyways is bathed in the glow of coloured lights, and entire families step out together to soak up the atmosphere, gaze at the huge nativity scene in Plaça Sant Jaume, and snack on cones of fragrant chestnuts roasted on braziers set up in the streets.

Right **Caga tió**

Pre-Christmas

Barcelona is teeming with shoppers leading up to Christmas. The main shopping streets – Passeig de Gràcia and the Rambla de Catalunya in L'Eixample, Portal de l'Angel in the Barri Gòtic – are especially lively, and sumptuously adorned, at this time of year, but for real atmosphere, head to the Fira de Santa Llúcia, the Christmas market that sprawls around the Gothic cathedral.

Christmas Gifts

Look out for the *caganer* (the 'crapper'), whose tiny squatting presence in every nativity scene ensures good luck in the year to come. You'll also see the *caga tió* ('crapping log' – are you seeing a pattern yet?), a stout branch leaning on two legs, one end painted with a smiley face and wearing a red *barretina* (traditional Catalan hat). The log is covered with a blanket and 'fed' every night before Christmas, when children beat it with sticks singing a charming little ditty that includes the words 'sh*t, log, sh*t'. The blanket is then whipped away and lo! The log has defecated a pile of sweets, nuts and small presents.

Christmas Dinner

A blow-out family meal usually happens on Christmas Eve (Nochebuena), and while turkey has become more popular in recent years, the classic feast involves a huge lump of meat slow-cooked for hours *(carn d'olla)*, and its stock served first as a soup *(escudella)*, into which are thrown large pasta shells known as *galets*. Any leftover meat is used for the cannelloni served on Sant Esteve (Boxing Day). Sea bass is also popular, along with a pile of shellfish and a large leg of cured ham, carved table-side.

Christmas Day

While elsewhere the usual drill is to spend Christmas with families and New Year with friends, in Spain it tends to be the reverse, and most bars and restaurants will be open, and full, on Christmas Day. Many will serve a set meal, although this is generally a slightly fancier version of their usual fare than any specific yuletide dishes. The streets are lively, as are the icy waters of the Port Vell, for the bracing annual harbour swim.

New Year

New Year's Eve kicks off with the Cursa dels Nassos, a not-entirely-serious half-marathon that attracts many thousands of participants. Later on dinner is normally eaten with family, but visitors will find most restaurants open, many serving a special menu – book well ahead if you can. As midnight approaches, check your underwear – you'll need to be wearing red for the best hope of a prosperous new year. You'll also need to come armed with 12 grapes, which you must stuff into your mouth at midnight, one grape for every stroke of the clock. The best place to do this is the Plaça Catalunya.

After that the fun really begins, and carries on well into the next day. Clubs tend not to get going until 2am or so, which gives you time to scour the bars for entrance flyers, without which admission can be a lot pricier than usual. Arriving before 2am will often get you in at a discount, too.

New Year's Day is a sleepy affair, aside from the brave souls plunging into the Mediterranean for the midday Primer Bany (First Swim) from the Club Natació Atlètic, free to all.

Turrón Temptation

At Christmas, specialist sweet stores fill with *turrón,* the traditional holiday temptation. Essentially nougat, it comes in different varieties: softer blocks are *turrón de Valencia* and a harder version is *turrón de Gijón*. You can find the treat year-round at stores such as Torrons Vicens, which has been selling its signature sweets since 1775.

Kings' Day

January 5th (Twelfth Night) is the day all good children look forward to (bad children can expect to find a lump of coal – nowadays generally made of sugar – at the foot of the bed). Round about 5pm, the Three Kings arrive at the port on a masted ship, where they are received by the mayor, and then slowly make their way around the city in a spectacular parade of floats, throwing armfuls of sweets over the expectant crowds. Their pages collect letters from the children containing wish lists of gifts – these are then delivered in the dead of night.

The following day (Dia de Reis) is a public holiday, and marks the end of the holiday season and the launch of the sales.

To read about:
La Familia see page 56
Spain's Religious Festivals see page 60

MADRID

The Golden Metropolis

Madrid is a miracle of human energy and peculiarly Spanish passions, a beguiling place with a simple message: this city knows how to live. It's a city whose contradictory impulses are legion, the perfect expression of Europe's most passionate country writ large. Madrid has transformed itself into one of Spain's premier style centres and its calling cards are many: astonishing art galleries, relentless nightlife, an exceptional live-music scene, a feast of fine restaurants and tapas bars, and a population that's mastered the art of the good life. It's not that other cities don't have these things: it's just that Madrid has all of them in bucketloads.

ARAPILES

RÍOS ROSAS

CASTELLANA

CHAMBERÍ

ARGÜELLES

TRAFALGAR

SALAMANCA

ALMAGRO

Parque del Oeste

CONDE DUQUE

La Rosaleda

MALASAÑA

RECOLETOS

Parque de la Montaña

CHUECA

Río Manzanares

JUSTICIA

Casa de Campo

CENTRO

RETIRO

Campo del Moro

CAMPO

LOS AUSTRIAS

SOL

Parque del Buen Retiro

HUERTAS

JERÓNIMOS

LA LATINA

ATOCHA

LAVAPIÈS

EL RASTRO

0   1 km
0   0.5 miles

Right **Puerta del Sol**

MADRID THROUGH THE EYES OF AN ARTIST

MADRID ART

Madrid isn't short of compelling reasons to visit. Visitors wax lyrical about beautiful plazas, tapas bars and the nightlife scene. But even if Madrid possessed none of these appealing attributes it would still retain one very good reason for spending as much time here as you can – its art, and the works of Goya in particular, which offer a window into the city's soul.

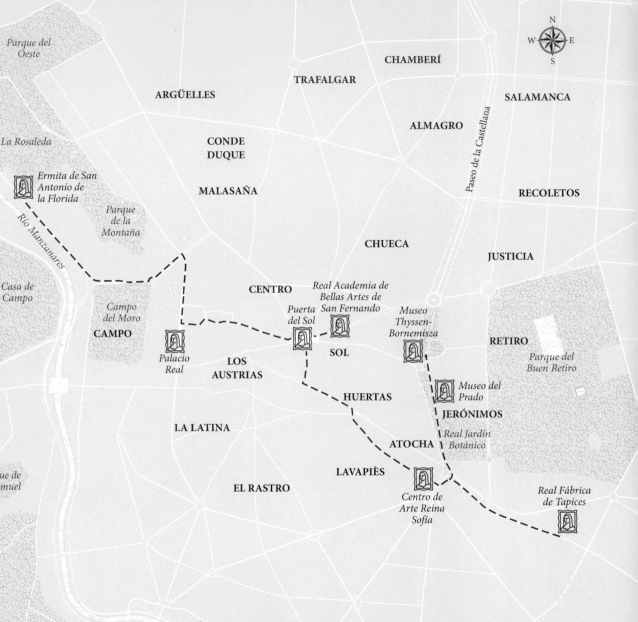

Parque del Oeste

La Rosaleda

Ermita de San Antonio de la Florida

Parque de la Montaña

ARGÜELLES

CONDE DUQUE

MALASAÑA

CHAMBERÍ

TRAFALGAR

ALMAGRO

SALAMANCA

Paseo de la Castellana

RECOLETOS

CHUECA

JUSTICIA

Casa de Campo

Campo del Moro

CAMPO

Palacio Real

LOS AUSTRIAS

CENTRO

Puerta del Sol

SOL

Real Academia de Bellas Artes de San Fernando

Museo Thyssen-Bornemisza

RETIRO

Parque del Buen Retiro

Museo del Prado

JERÓNIMOS

HUERTAS

Real Jardín Botánico

LA LATINA

Parque de Caramuel

EL RASTRO

LAVAPIÈS

ATOCHA

Centro de Arte Reina Sofía

Real Fábrica de Tapices

Parque de San Isidro

Río Manzanares

0   1 km
0   0.5 miles

This relatively young capital (it only became the national seat of government in 1561) may be short on history, but more than makes up for it in the richness of the art its galleries hold. Dozens of collections, large and small, can be found across the city but there are three specific museums – the Museo del Prado, the Museo Thyssen-Bornemisza and the Centro de Arte Reina Sofía – that draw the biggest crowds.

The three points of this Golden Triangle of art sit within a short walk of each other along or just off elegant Paseo de la Castellana, Madrid's main thoroughfare. All have show-stopping masterpieces from the greatest artists who ever put paint to canvas, but the highlight for many visitors is the work of home-grown genius, Francisco José de Goya y Lucientes (1746–1828). His astute observations, irreverent approach and candid depictions of horrific events he lived through make his work the quintessential window into Madrid life in the late 18th and early 19th centuries.

Once you've enjoyed the museums themselves, the city has links to Goya and his fellow artists that help form a greater understanding of the paintings, giving a historical context to both the pieces and the people who produced them.

Nobody should leave Madrid without experiencing the unrivalled art to be found in this world-class cultural city.

Museo del Prado

Exploring the Prado, Madrid's premier gallery, could take days, such is the quality and breadth of the collection. The focus is on Spanish painters, and the strongest card in the Prado's artful deck is the work by Goya and artists such as Diego Velázquez who influenced him.

**Left Detail of *Las meninas*
(The Maids of Honour) by Velázquez**

Velázquez' most celebrated painting, *Las meninas* (The Maids of Honour), was completed in 1656 and depicts not only King Philip IV, his wife and his daughter, but also the artist himself. It's an enigmatic portrait thanks to its composition and use of light, which has confounded and delighted admirers over the centuries. Painted 150 years later, Goya's *La familia de Carlos IV* (The Family of Charles IV) is a homage to his artistic predecessor. Like Velázquez, Goya inserted himself into the artwork but, typically for this unorthodox painter, he gave a less-than-flattering portrayal of the monarchy.

His rebellious palette had darker tones too, best seen in the late-career *Pinturas negras* (Black Paintings) with their terrifying themes of demonic ceremonies and gruesome cannibalism. The loss of his hearing and the horrors of the French occupation of Spain ultimately led to these sombre works, and the latter was also the inspiration for two of his most celebrated paintings: *El dos de mayo* (The Second of May, aka The Charge of the Mamelukes) and *El tres de mayo* (The Third of May) show the people of Madrid rebelling against French forces and the violent retaliation of the invaders.

Museo Thyssen-Bornemisza
Just across from the Prado, the Museo Thyssen-Bornemisza is one of the most extraordinary private collections of predominantly European art in the world.

Here, beneath one roof, are works from seemingly every European painter of distinction, from 13th-century religious art to zany 21st-century creations. There may just be one painting, or a handful of paintings from each artist, but the Thyssen is the place to immerse yourself in an astonishing range of artistic styles.

Real Fábrica de Tapices
A 20-minute walk south, past the Botanic Garden, leads to the Royal Tapestry Factory. It was here that the young Goya cut his artistic teeth in 1774 after moving to Madrid from his home in Aragón. Asked to help with designs for royal-commissioned tapestries, the patterns he drew, many based on paintings by Velázquez, caught the king's eye and launched the artist's career. Today, tours include rooms filled with tapestries, some for sale, and the chance to see them made.

Centro de Arte Reina Sofía
As Goya recorded the brutalities of 18th-century warfare, so another Spanish artist, Picasso, set down in paint the barbarity of a 20th-century conflict, the Spanish Civil War. *Guernica,* his disturbing, moving piece created in response to the devastating aerial bombardment of the eponymous Basque town in 1937, is the highlight of the Reina Sofía and a worthy successor to Goya's war paintings.

This gallery of modern art, the southern tip of the Golden Triangle, is housed in a former convent and is home to famous works by the likes of Miró and Dalí – but it is Picasso's haunting depiction of suffering that lingers most in the memory after a visit.

Puerta del Sol
A 15-minute walk northwest, through the heart of Madrid, leads to the city's geographical and spiritual home, Puerta del Sol. Today a transport and shopping hub, where people celebrate New Year's Eve and from where all road distances from the capital are measured (look for the south side), this is also where the violent events depicted in Goya's *El dos de mayo* took place. It's still possible to imagine the brave local population fighting at extremely close quarters with the French Mameluke troops in the square and narrow surrounding streets.

Real Academia de Bellas Artes de San Fernando
To the northeast is the Royal Academy of Fine Arts, one of Spain's most prestigious art schools and a place with which Picasso, as one of its students, was very familiar. Or at least he would have been had he chosen to spend more time here during the two years he lived in Madrid.

Instead young Pablo preferred learning firsthand from the Old Masters, spending his time in the Prado admiring the likes of Goya, who was one of the early directors of the academy. Thirteen pieces by Goya are on display inside, including self-portraits, and portraits of King Fernando VII and the infamous minister Manuel Godoy.

Palacio Real
A short stroll west through the streets of Madrid's medieval quarter brings you to the Royal Palace. The current building was constructed in 1734 after a fire destroyed the earlier Moorish fortress turned regal abode that Velázquez would have visited. Some 74 years later this was the starting point of the May rebellion, when crowds gathered outside to protest the influence of France over the country.

The opulent palace is no longer home to the Spanish royals, but official functions are still held here. The square in

Right Centro de Arte Reina Sofía

front offers expansive views: look across the Río Manzanares and to the left – today you'll see the Puerta del Angel neighbourhood, but two centuries ago this is where Goya's house stood.

La Quinta del Sordo (Deaf Man's Villa, named after an earlier deaf owner, not Goya) is where the artist created his *Pinturas negras*, executed directly onto the walls of his home, where they remained until the villa was demolished in 1909 and the paintings were moved to the Prado.

Ermita de San Antonio de la Florida

Northwest of the Palacio Real (through Plaza de Oriente with its gravity-defying, Velázquez-designed statue of Phillip IV) is this off-the-beaten-track church. Not only is it home to magnificent frescoes by Goya, but it's also the painter's final resting place. His body (minus the mysteriously missing head) lies in front of the altar, placed here after it was returned from France where he died in 1828.

To read about:

Master of Illusion: Salvador Dalí see page 170
The Natural Art of Lanzarote see page 212

OLDEST RESTAURANT IN THE WORLD

MADRID FOOD & DRINK

It's not every day that you can eat in the oldest restaurant in the world, but Restaurante Sobrino de Botín (opened in 1725 and recognised by the Guinness Book of Records) claims the title. The secret of its staying power is fine cochinillo asado (roast suckling pig) and cordero asado (roast lamb) cooked in wood-fired ovens. Eating in the vaulted cellar is a treat.

Roasted Meats

Madrid shares with much of
the Spanish interior a love of roasted
meats. More specifically, *asado de
cordero lechal* (spring lamb roasted
in a wood-fired oven) is a winter obsession in Madrid just as it is on much
of the surrounding meseta of central
Spain. Usually served with roasted
potatoes (it's customary to also order
a green salad to accompany the lamb
and lighten things up a little), it's a
mainstay in many of Madrid's more
traditional restaurants. Less celebrated (it's all relative) is *cochinillo asado*
(roast suckling pig) from the Segovia
region northwest of Madrid.

The restaurant occupies four storeys of
a historic building just outside of Plaza
Mayor. If you call ahead, you can book a
table in the bodega – the oldest part of
the building, built in the 15th century.

The restaurant has also appeared in
many novels about Madrid, most notably
Ernest Hemingway's *The Sun Also Rises*
and Frederick Forsyth's *Icon* and *The
Cobra*.

Yes, it's filled with tourists. And yes,
staff are keen to keep things ticking over
and there's little chance to linger. But the
novelty value is high and the food excellent.

To read about:
Jamón Jamón see page 48
The Hour of Vermouth see page 272

HANDMADE IN MADRID

MADRID ARTS & CRAFTS

Madrid is a city that seems to run on a soundtrack of Spanish guitar. You hear it everywhere: humming from cafe radios and car stereos, drifting from windows, seeping under the doorways of bars. Buskers hammer out flamenco tunes on the street corners, while bands drift from bar to bar, serenading drinkers with songs of lust, love, loss and longing. But guitar making is not the only traditional craft still surviving in Madrid.

Classical Guitars

For Spanish people, there's something special about the sound of the guitar, according to Amalia Ramírez, whose family has been making fine classical guitars since 1882. 'It has an expressive tone, full of emotion, and conveys a passion few other instruments can', she explains. 'It's the sound of the Spanish soul.'

Founded by and named after Amalia's great-great-great-grandfather, José Ramírez has been the luthier of choice for many of the 20th century's top guitarists – including George Harrison, Eric Clapton and Andrés Segovia, perhaps the greatest of classical guitarists. While each generation has honed the Ramírez design, the basics of their guitars have remained essentially unchanged for a century.

The Ramírez workshop is tucked away on a shady backstreet in Madrid's Tetuán district. Inside, craftspeople lean over workbenches, and bits of half-completed guitars line the walls – trusses, braces, headstocks and soundboards – along with finished instruments awaiting a final polish before being shipped out to their owners.

There are no shortcuts to making a great guitar. Each instrument has the same basic design but many factors affect its tone: the type of wood, the finish, the hand of the artisan who makes it. And because they're all originals, each has its own character. 'That's the difference between something handmade and something mass-produced', Amalia explains. 'And that's why they cost more.'

Guitar making by hand is a long and laborious process. Each guitar takes around four months to complete, and only 50 or 60 are made in the workshop every year. As a result, they can command eye-watering prices – from a couple of thousand euros for basic models up to tens of thousands for custom designs.

Spanish Capes

Guitar making is just one of many old crafts which live on in Madrid. On Calle de la Cruz, Capas Seseña is the only place in Spain that still makes the heavy woollen cloak known as the *capa española*, a garment traditionally worn for formal occasions such as bullfights or nights at the theatre. Each cape consists of a 5m circle of Salamancan wool, cut and sewn by hand.

The feel of the shop is deliberately old-fashioned: framed photographs of clients line the boutique downstairs, beside hundreds of capes suspended from brass clothing rails, while seamstresses work in the upstairs studio, surrounded by swathes of cloth and dressmakers' mannequins.

Traditionally, capes were only worn by men and came in just three colours (blue, black and brown), but these days capes are designed for women too, in brighter colours and lighter fabrics. A Capas Seseña cape has always been an exclusive product: Michael Jackson owned one, Hillary Clinton has one in her wardrobe, and Pablo Picasso liked his so much he was buried in it.

Flamenco Shoes

For flamenco aficionados, the name of Don Flamenco commands a similar cachet. For decades, this streetside cobbler on Calle León is where the city's dancers have come to buy their *zapatos de flamenco* (flamenco shoes). Each pair is still finished by hand by Don Flamenco himself. Dressed in an old apron and spectacles, and surrounded by old tools, he buffs the leather, polishes the shoes to a sheen, and finally taps hobnails into the heels and toes – the crucial design feature which allows the dancers to produce the distinctive flamenco tap.

Made with Love

Back at José Ramírez, Amalia explains the continuing appeal of Madrid's craft tradition. 'I think we often forget the value of handmade things', she says. 'When something's been made by a craftsman with love and skill, there's a beauty to it that you can almost touch.'

To read about:
Madrid Through the Eyes of an Artist see page 264
Oldest Restaurant in the World see page 268

SUNDAY AFTERNOON: THE HOUR OF VERMOUTH

Madrileños love their Sundays, and although there are numerous variations on the theme, they usually go something like this. The day begins in the morning (early or otherwise) at the flea market of El Rastro, before the masses fan out into the bars of La Latina to order a vermouth at 1pm for la hora del vermut *(vermouth hour).*

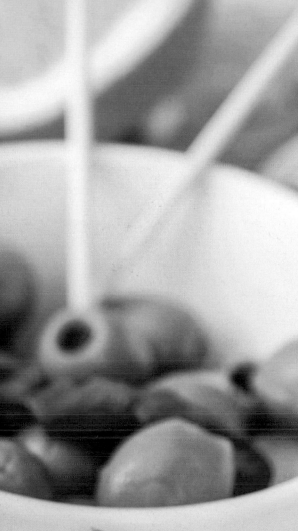

El Rastro

A Sunday morning at El Rastro flea market is a Madrid institution. You could easily spend an entire morning inching your way down the hill and the maze of streets. Cheap clothes, luggage, old flamenco records, even older photos of Madrid, faux designer purses, grungy T-shirts, household goods and electronics are the main fare. For every 10 pieces of junk, there's a real gem (a lost masterpiece, an Underwood typewriter) waiting to be found.

The crowded Sunday flea market was, back in the 17th and 18th centuries, largely a meat market (*rastro* means 'stain', in reference to the trail of blood left behind by animals dragged down the hill). The road leading through the market, Calle de la Ribera de los Curtidores, translates as 'Tanners' Alley' and further evokes this sense of a slaughterhouse past. On Sunday mornings this is the place to be, with seemingly all of Madrid (in all its diversity) here in search of a bargain.

La Hora del Vermut

One o'clock Sunday afternoon. A dark bar off Calle de la Cava Baja. In any civilised city the bar would be shut tight, but in Madrid the place is packed because it's *la hora del vermut,* a long-standing tradition whereby friends and families head out for a quick aperitif before Sunday lunch. Sometimes referred to as *ir de Rastro* (going to the Rastro) because so many of the traditional vermouth bars are in and around El Rastro market, this Sunday tradition is deeply ingrained in *madrileño* culture. The legendary tavern Casa Alberto is an atmospheric place to take part.

Some of the best bars for vermouth are along La Latina's Calle de la Cava Baja in La Latina. One of the most important gastronomic streets in Spain, it is lined with tapas bars. Some have elevated these tiny morsels into art forms, others serve up specialities in traditional clay pots. Such is Madrid's love affair with tapas and the culture of enjoying them that even this long and graceful thoroughfare cannot contain the neighbourhood's tapas offerings. Nearby you'll find Madrid's best *tortilla de patatas* (potato omelette) at Juana La Loca or Txirimiri.

Parque del Buen Retiro

Later, many gather in the Parque del Buen Retiro to do everything from reading the Sunday papers, taking a boat ride on the lake or falling asleep (or all of the above), to having a picnic or waiting for the drum circle that starts banging out rhythms on Sunday evenings.

The glorious gardens of El Retiro are as beautiful as any you'll find in a European city. Littered with marble monuments, landscaped lawns, the occasional elegant building (the Palacio de Cristal is especially worth seeking out) and abundant greenery, it's quiet and contemplative during the week but comes to life on weekends. Put simply, this is one of the best places in Madrid.

To read about:

Tortilla: Spanish Omelette see page 66
La Siesta: The Art of Napping see page 86

SUNSET AT TEMPLO DE DEBOD

Yes, that is an Egyptian temple in downtown Madrid. No matter which way you look at it, there's something incongruous about finding the Templo de Debod in the Parque de la Montaña northwest of Plaza de España. The temple was saved from the rising waters of Lake Nasser in southern Egypt when Egyptian president Gamal Abdel Nasser built the Aswan High Dam. After 1968 it was sent block by block to Spain as a gesture of thanks to Spanish archaeologists in the Unesco team that worked to save the monuments that would otherwise have disappeared forever.

To read about:

KILLING
THE NIGHT

Nights in the Spanish capital are the stuff of legend. They're invariably long and loud most nights of the week, rising to a deafening crescendo as the weekend nears. And what Ernest Hemingway wrote of the city in the 1930s remains true to this day: 'Nobody goes to bed in Madrid until they have killed the night'.

Right **Nightlife on Calle de Cádiz**

Madrid is said to have more bars per capita than any other city in Europe, and, wherever you are in town, there'll be a bar close by. But bars are only half the story. On any night in Madrid, drinks, tapas and wines segue easily into cocktail bars and the nightclubs that have brought such renown to Madrid as the unrivalled scene of all-night fiestas.

Huertas

Surely it was the *barrio* (district) of Huertas that Ernest Hemingway had in mind when he famously coined the phrase about killing the Madrid night. The noise from Huertas at night crackles across the city like the clamour of an approaching storm, and watching the day break over the *barrio*'s Plaza de Santa Ana is something of a Madrid rite of passage.

Right on the square, Cerveceria Alemana was a Hemingway favourite and it still serves its own beer along the same wood-lined bar. Just across the square is Villa Rosa, now a respected venue for live flamenco, where you'll wonder if you've strayed into the craziness of a Pedro Almodóvar film: Villa Rosa's facade appears in *Tacones lejanos* (High Heels).

But it's the riffing sound of jazz that is the *barrio*'s true mark of musical distinction. In Café Central, on Calle de las Huertas, serious aficionados nod in time to the blend of classic and Latin jazz (Madrid's been one of Europe's jazz capitals since the 1920s). Other jazz bars ripple out across the neighbourhood, while down the bottom of the Huertas hill, La Dolores and the eclectic Los Gatos are mainstays of the night.

But if Huertas has one true icon, it is La Venezia, an old-style sherry bar where they pour this southern Spanish classic straight from the barrel.

La Latina

La Latina is Madrid's best *barrio* for tapas. If you're planning only one tapas crawl while in town, do it here in Calle de la Cava Baja and surrounding streets. Most nights (and Sunday afternoons), it's filled with a discerning crowd of twenty- and thirty-something urban sophisticates, who ensure that there's little room to move in the good places and that the bad ones don't survive long. Many of these places are better known for their tapas, but they're equally great for a drink.

At Almendro 13 you can eat like a king – if the king in question is, like Spain's Juan Carlos I, a man of uncomplicated tastes. Its speciality, and the king's favourite, is the simple *huevos rotos* (broken eggs) – a fried egg atop potato slices and Spanish ham. Here *madrileños* elbow their way to the bar and, seemingly with one voice, order *huevos rotos*. Thereafter they retire to rest said elbows on the upturned barrels and eat their dish with satisfaction.

The tapas at Juana la Loca are somewhat more fancy. All along the bar, *gulas* (baby eels) cascade from vivid lime-green spinach crepes, and long shavings of courgettes wrap delicately around cod, tiny capsicums and onion. But Juana la Loca's signature dish is the *tortilla de patatas* (potato omelette). By caramelising the onions, nothing more, Juana la Loca's chefs have achieved that rare miracle – developing a following among *madrileños* for a tortilla that wasn't cooked by their *abuelas* (grandmothers).

La Movida Madrileña

After the long, dark years of dictatorship and conservative Catholicism, Spaniards, especially those in Madrid, emerged onto the streets as Spain returned to democracy in the late 1970s. Nothing was taboo in the phenomenon known as *la movida* (the scene) or *la movida madrileña* (the Madrid scene), as young Spaniards discovered the '60s, '70s and early '80s all at once. All-night partying was the norm, drug taking in public was not a criminal offence and Madrid in particular howled. Summer terraces roared to the chattering, drinking, carousing crowds, and young people from all over Europe (not to mention cultural icons such as Andy Warhol) flocked to join the revelry.

La movida was also an explosion of creativity among the country's musicians, designers and film-makers. The most famous of these was director Pedro Almodóvar, whose riotously colourful films featured larger-than-life characters who pushed the limits of sex and drugs. Although his later films became internationally renowned, his first films, *Pepi, Luci, Bom y otras chicas del montón* (Pepi, Luci, Bom and the Other Girls; 1980) and *Laberinto de pasiones* (Labyrinth of Passion; 1982) are where the spirit of the movement really comes alive. Other important cultural figures to emerge from *la movida* include fashion designer Agatha Ruiz de la Prada and film director Fernando Trueba.

Every person you meet along Calle de la Cava Baja is a passionate defender of his or her favourite tapas haunt. But a consensus finally builds around Txakolina, a Basque place with walls of discarded wine cartons. The bar's motto is 'high cuisine in miniature'. Not far away, at wine bars like Taberna Tempranillo and Bonanno, the focus is more on the drinking, while keeping small tapas plates before you to make sure you last the night.

Chueca

Chueca is Madrid's rebellious teen that grew up and got stylish. In the 1980s, Chueca wholeheartedly surrendered its soul to *'la movida madrileña',* the city's decade-long cultural awakening and celebration of Spain's post-dictatorship freedom. At the time, the *New York Times* dubbed Madrid 'the cultural capital of the world'. And when the party ran its course, the young professionals of Madrid's gay community moved in, transforming Chueca from a neglected inner-city space into one of the city's most stylish, most culture-conscious *barrios*. By day, you'll find the majority of Madrid's private contemporary art galleries here. By night, the city becomes a byword for the sort of joyful hedonism for which Madrid is famed.

The epicentre of the *barrio's* nightly fiesta is the Plaza de Chueca, with some of Madrid's most storied bars clustered nearby, among them Antigua Casa Ángel Sierra and Café Acuarela. Nearby, Baco y Beto is a terrific tapas bar, while Café Belén serves up the city's best mojitos.

Cocktail bars abound along Calle de la Reina and Gran Vía. There are many candidates for the title of Madrid's best cocktail bar, but none come close to Museo Chicote. The founder of this Madrid landmark (complete with 1930s-era interior) is said to have invented more than 100 cocktails, which the likes of Ernest Hemingway, Ava Gardner, Grace Kelly, Sophia Loren and Frank Sinatra have all enjoyed at one time or another. It's at its best after midnight, when a lounge atmosphere takes over, couples cuddle on the curved benches and some of the city's best DJs do their stuff.

Chamberí

Heading north, as you leave behind central Madrid's tangle of sometimes claustrophobic streets, you'll start to breathe more freely: the streets are wider and life appears to slow down. Plaza de Olavide is the green hub of Chamberí life, looking and sounding for all the world like a village square in rural Spain. By night, the plaza's soundtrack increases in volume as locals crowd the outdoor tables of the surrounding bars. Inside one of these, Bar Méntrida, you'll find a stirring photographic record of the plaza's history.

Northeast of the plaza, on Calle de Santa Engracia, behind the extravagantly tiled facade of another iconic Chamberí bar, Bodega de la Ardosa, lies another world. Opened in 1919 as a bodega (wine cellar), La Ardosa has been left largely unchanged in the years since. In contrast to its stunning facade, which is pockmarked by shrapnel holes from the days of the Spanish Civil War, La Ardosa's walls are adorned with tiles of the kind that graced the bathroom of many a Spanish *abuela* c 1965. Bottles gathering dust line the shelves and *barrio* old-timers and young local workers wander in and out, oblivious to the paper napkins strewn on the floor.

Nearby Calle de Ponzano is fast becoming the hottest night-time ticket in the new Madrid, lined as it is with innovative tapas and wine bars that are filled to bursting every night of the week.

To read about:
Sipping Sherry in Jerez see page 94
Oldest Restaurant in the World see page 268

Left Mercado de San Miguel

Index

Image Credits

Behind the Scenes

Associate Product Director Kirsten Rawlings
Series Designer Campbell McKenzie
Senior Product Editor Grace Dobell
Cartographic Designer Wayne Murphy
Book Designer Wibowo Rusli
Product Editor Jenna Myers
Senior Cartographer Corey Hutchison
Cover Researcher Naomi Parker

Written by Andrew Bain, Sarah Baxter, Oliver Bennett, Oliver Berry, Matt Bolton, Gregor Clark, Lucy Corne, Sally Davies, Esme Fox, Duncan Garwood, Anthony Ham, Ben Handicott, Anita Isalska, Christa Larwood, Catherine Le Nevez, Fionnuala McCarthy, Isabella Noble, John Noble, Stephanie Ong, Jheni Osman, Javier Panero, Lorna Parkes, Josephine Quintero, Sarah Reid, Kalya Ryan, Brendan Sainsbury, Oliver Smith, Tom Stainer, Regis St Louis, Andy Symington, Giles Tremlett, Clifton Wilkinson, Lonely Planet Travel News (www.lonelyplanet.com/news)

Thanks to Ronan Abayawickrema, Will Allen, Imogen Bannister, Bridget Blair, Jennifer Carey, Anna Carroll, Hannah Cartmel, Heather Champion, Kate Chapman, Gwen Cotter, Shona Gray, James Hardy, Andi Jones, Sandie Kestell, Kate Kiely, Neil Manders, Anne Mason, Virginia Moreno, Darren O'Connell, Mazzy Prinsep, Alison Ridgway, Kathryn Rowan, James Smart, Lyahna Spencer, Gabrielle Stefanos, Saralinda Turner, Amanda Williamson, Juan Winata

Published by Lonely Planet Global Limited
CRN 554153

1st edition – April 2019
ISBN 9781788682657

© Lonely Planet 2019
Photographs © as indicated 2019
Printed in China
10 9 8 7 6 5 4 3 2 1

LONELY PLANET OFFICES

Australia
The Malt Store, Level 3, 551 Swanston Street, Carlton, VIC 3053
Phone 03 8379 8000

United Kingdom
240 Blackfriars Road, London SE1 8NW
Phone 020 3771 5100

USA
124 Linden St, Oakland, CA 94607
Phone 510 250 6400

Ireland
Digital Depot, Roe Lane (off Thomas St), Digital Hub, Dublin 8, D08 TCV4

STAY IN TOUCH lonelyplanet.com/contact